Editor
Lorin Klistoff, M.A.

Managing Editor
Karen Goldfluss, M.S. Ed.

Editor-in-Chief
Sharon Coan, M.S. Ed.

Illustrator
Kathy Marlin

Cover Artist
Brenda DiAntonis

Art Director
CJae Froshay

Imaging
Ralph Olmedo, Jr.

Product Manager
Phil Garcia

Product Developer
Quack & Co.

Publishers
Rachelle Cracchiolo, M.S. Ed.
Mary Dupuy Smith, M.S. Ed.

Building Christian Character

Love
Caring
Responsibility
Self-Control
Patience
Forgiveness
Honoring God

Written by
Robin Wolfe

Teacher Created Materials, Inc.
6421 Industry Way
Westminster, CA 92683
www.teachercreated.com
ISBN-0-7439-7103-5
©2002 Teacher Created Materials, Inc.
Reprinted, 2004
Made in U.S.A.

Table of Contents

Introduction

Building Christian character in our children is an important task. Teachers and parents will find this book to be a valuable resource in accomplishing that goal. Children will discover that learning good values can be fun!

This book contains 13 units, each unit focusing on a different value. Children will learn about honoring God, obeying rules, telling the truth, and other values that help to build Christian character.

Each unit contains a teacher's resource page that supplies ideas for games, crafts, object lessons, and simple songs. Complete, simple instructions for each activity, as well as illustrations, make teaching easy. A Bible story is provided to teach each value lesson. Questions at the end of the story will provide an opportunity for the children to think about what the story means and how to apply it.

There are reproducible activity pages for the children that reinforce the lessons. Puzzles, mazes, word searches, and other interesting activities will stimulate the children's imaginations. Also included are application stories about children who are learning to build Christian character. A contract page helps the children make a commitment to practice the good values that they have learned.

In addition, an answer key for the activity pages is provided at the end of the book.

Each week, encourage the children to think about what the world would be like if everyone had Christian values. Look for opportunities to model good values to the children as you are teaching. Be sure to praise the children for their efforts to build Christian character in their own lives!

Use bright colors to color the letters above. Try to make the picture look like a stained glass window.

To honor God means . . .

- to believe in Him
- to love Him
- to worship Him
- to admire Him
- to praise Him
- to value Him

- to think very highly of Him
- to behave reverently toward Him
- to use His name respectfully
- to obey His commands

Activities for Honoring God

The activities below are a fun way to get children into the habit of praising and honoring God each day.

Craft: Make a Collage

Provide magazines or old catalogs for the children. Have the children find pictures of things God has given them. Remind them that God takes care of all their needs. He also gives extra things that are just for fun. Tell the children to find and cut out pictures of some of these things, and glue them onto a large sheet of paper or posterboard. Have them label their posters "God Gives Great Gifts." Read Matthew 7:9–11 to the children. Discuss the verses.

Game: Keep It Going

Have the children sit in a circle with you. Tell them that they are going to honor God by thinking of some nice things to say about Him. Explain that they will be taking turns creating sentences honoring God. Tell the children that each child can only say one word. The person who starts the sentence will always say, "God." Then the next person adds a word to the sentence, and so on, until the sentence is finished. Then another sentence can be started. For example, child 1 says "God." Child 2 says, "made." Child 3 says "the." Child 4 says "world," "animals," or a different word. Explain to the children that they won't know what the sentence is going to be at first. They'll have to just keep adding to it until it is a complete sentence honoring God.

Song

(tune: "Jesus Loves Me")

I will honor God today.
I will honor God this way:
Sing His praises all my days;
Use His name in reverent ways.

Yes, I will praise Him.
Yes, I will praise Him.
Yes, I will praise Him.
I want to honor Him.

Unit
1

Two Missionaries Honor God

In the New Testament, we can read about two men named Paul and Barnabas. They were missionaries. They traveled from town to town and country to country preaching the good news that Jesus, the Son of God, died on the cross to save people from their sins. Sometimes they performed miracles with the power that God gave them.

One day, Paul and Barnabas went to a town called Lystra. They saw a man there who was crippled in his feet. He had been that way since he was born. He had never been able to walk. Paul looked at the man and called out, "Stand on your feet!" And guess what happened—the man not only stood up, he jumped up! He could walk!

When the crowd saw what Paul had done, they shouted, "The gods have come down to us in human form!" The reason the people said that was because they believed in many false gods. They thought that Paul was a god named Hermes and that Barnabas was a god named Zeus. They brought bulls to the city gates to offer sacrifices to Paul and Barnabas and worshipped them.

(Continued on the next page.)

Unit 1

Two Missionaries Honor God

When Paul and Barnabas found out that the people intended to worship them, they rushed into the crowd and shouted, "Why are you doing this? We are only men, human like you." Paul and Barnabas did not allow the people to honor them for healing the crippled man. They knew that it was God who had really healed him.

Then Paul and Barnabas honored God by giving Him all the credit. They told the crowd about God. They said, "We are bringing you good news, telling you to turn from these worthless idols to the living God, who made heaven and earth and sea and everything in them." They went on to tell the people that it is God who shows kindness to them by sending them rain for their crops, and providing food for them. They even told them that God is the one who fills their hearts with joy!

Paul and Barnabas could have taken the credit for healing the crippled man. They could have let the people worship and honor them, but that would have been wrong. Instead, they praised God and told the people about Him. They made a choice to honor God!

Talk About It

- Paul and Barnabas gave God the credit for making the crippled man walk—even though people thought Paul did it. They honored God. Tell about a time when you gave credit to God and honored Him.

- What is a miracle? Humans can't make a miracle happen. Who can?

- How do you think the crippled man felt when he found he could walk?

- How could he have honored God?

Unit 1

Jesus Honors God

Name _____

Jesus knows it is important to honor God. He honored God by doing what God sent Him to do—to die on the cross to save us from our sins! Then God honored Jesus by raising Him from the dead and giving Him a throne in heaven!

A secret message is hidden in the puzzle below. To find it, use a dark crayon or marker to color in every box containing a number or an animal word. When you are finished, some words will be left over and a special shape will appear! Read the words in the shape in order. It is something that Jesus wants us to do to honor God.

30	7	pig	"'Love	12	sheep	frog
horse	1	dog	the	47	9	3
cow	cat	5	Lord	16	camel	elephant
2	goat	99	your	rabbit	10	mouse
God	with	all	your	heart	and	with
hippo	11	giraffe	all	20	4	fox
15	buffalo	rat	your	65	tiger	0
deer	wolf	13	soul	80	raccoon	zebra
7	58	lion	and	19	lizard	leopard
donkey	squirrel	6	with	41	8	turtle
bear	300	hog	all	mule	75	17
snake	beaver	skunk	your	22	600	38
gorilla	cheetah	50	mind.'"	monkey	panda	311

Unit 1

Psalms to Honor God

Name _____

Reading the book of Psalms is a good way to
find out how to praise and honor God. Read
the verses from Psalms and the clues in
parentheses. Find the answers in the balloons.
Write them on the lines.

1. Let all the __ __ __ __ __ (our planet)
   $\overline{11}$

   fear the Lord; let all the __ __ __ __ __
   $\overline{8}$

   (human beings) of the world __ __ __ __ __ __
   $\overline{3}$

   (honor, esteem) him. (Psalm 33:8)

2. __ __ __ __ __ (Yell) for joy to the Lord, all the
   $\overline{12}$ $\overline{6}$

   __ __ __ __ __ (our planet). Worship the Lord
   $\overline{7}$

   with __ __ __ __ __ __ __ __ (happiness);
   $\overline{1}$ $\overline{9}$

   come before him with joyful __ __ __ __ __
   $\overline{5}$ $\overline{10}$

   (tunes). Know that the Lord is __ __ __ (Jesus'
   $\overline{2}$

   Father). It is he who __ __ __ __ (created) us,
   $\overline{4}$

   and we are his . . . (Psalm 100:1–3)

Balloons: made, God, songs, earth, Shout, revere, people, gladness, earth

Now write the letters in the blanks below that match the numbers in your
answers above.

3. I __ __ __ __ you, O Lord, my __ __ __ __ __ __ __ __.
   1 2 3 4   5 6 7 8 9 10 11 12

   (Psalm 18:1)

Get a Clue, Kyle!

Kyle was the most popular boy in school. Everyone liked him. He was good-looking, smart, and funny. At recess, the boys fought over who would get Kyle on their football team. He was tough and could run fast. He was a good athlete, and everyone knew it. Kyle had lots of trophies at home that he had won in the city sports league.

At the class picnic on the last day of school, Kyle and the other boys found a grassy area where they could play football. Because it was a warm day, the boys stopped to rest after they had played a little while. Kyle said, "Hey, let's choose teams and make our own neighborhood football league for the summer. We could meet at the park every morning next week and practice!" The guys all yelled, "Yeah, great idea!"

Then Kenny remembered that Vacation Bible School would start next week at church. It would be held in the mornings. He and his sisters planned to go. He said, "Oh, wait, I can't come in the mornings next week. I'm going to Vacation Bible School."

Kyle laughed and said, "You go to Bible School? Oh, brother, that's just for sissies. I never go to church, and I sure wouldn't spend a whole week in the summer going to Vacation Bible School. That's dumb."

Kenny looked a little uncomfortable, but then he said, "Well, look, instead of practicing in the mornings, why don't we just practice in the afternoons? I can come then!"

(Continued on the next page.)

Unit 1

Get a Clue, Kyle!

Kyle used God's name like it was a bad word. He said, "You're such a baby. You'd rather go to church than play football? You've got to be kidding."

Sam and Dusty were disappointed that Kyle was making fun of Kenny for going to Bible school. They also didn't like it when Kyle used God's name in a bad way. Sam said, "Kyle, I agree with Kenny. We can just play in the afternoons. And I don't think it's sissy to go to Vacation Bible School. Our church has it in July, and I plan to go!"

Dusty spoke up, too. "I go to Vacation Bible School every summer in another town when I go to my grandma and grandpa's. I like it! It's fun! You learn interesting stories about the Bible and about God. Kyle, you ought to try it. Maybe you would have fun, too!"

Then a couple of other boys said, "Oh, come on, Kyle, let's just practice in the afternoons."

Kenny felt so much better when Sam and Dusty spoke up and agreed with him. The other boys all looked at Kyle. Kyle could see he was outnumbered. He said, "Ok, we'll practice in the afternoons, I guess. But everyone better be here by one o'clock on the dot!"

"We will," said the boys. Everyone ran back on the field to start playing their game again. Sam and Dusty went up to Kenny and "high-fived" him. They felt good that they had found a way to play football and still honor God, too!

Talk About It

- What might have happened if Sam and Dusty hadn't spoken up?
- How do you think God feels about Kyle's attitude?
- How do you think God feels about what Kenny, Sam, and Dusty said?
- If someone makes fun of you for going to church, what should you do?

Unit 1

What Would You Do?

Name _____

Read each situation below. In the box, write or draw what you would do to honor God.

1. You are watching a TV show. The story is funny, and you like the people on the show. One of the characters, however, keeps using God's name in a bad way. What would you do to honor God?

2. Your soccer team is tied for first place. The big play-off game that will decide the championship is scheduled for Sunday morning at the same time as worship services. The coach lectures everyone on being committed to the team and how important it is to be there for the game. What would you do to honor God?

3. You and your best friend go to the grocery store with your mom. While your mom is standing in line to pay for her groceries, she realizes that she forgot to buy cereal. She tells you and your friend to stay in line while she goes to get it. Your friend points to the candy rack then secretly slips a candy bar in your pocket. You don't want to make your best friend mad, but you know that God says it is wrong to steal. What would you do to honor God?

Unit 1

My Contract

Name _____

Put a √ by the actions below that you can do to honor God. Put an X by the actions that you should NOT do in order to honor God.

____ Sing praises.

____ Use God's name in a bad way.

____ Attend church services.

____ Invite someone to church.

____ Ignore God.

____ Tell others about Jesus.

____ Behave in Bible class.

____ Break God's rules.

____ Tell lies.

____ Read the Bible.

____ Pray.

____ Worship God.

____ Make fun of God.

____ Love God.

Reading your Bible honors God. Find Revelation 4:11. It is near the end of your Bible. Fill in the blanks to finish this Bible verse that honors God.

"You are worthy, our Lord and _____,

to receive _____ and

_____ and power, for you

_____ all things . . ."

If you want to make a commitment to honor God, copy the sentence below. Then sign your name and write the date.

I promise to do my best to honor God every day.

_____

_____

Signed _____

Date _____

Respect Others

To help you practice respecting the rights of other people, work with a classmate to follow these directions. Using one yellow crayon and one green crayon, take turns coloring every other letter green. Color the other letters yellow. Can you and your classmate figure out a way to be fair and take turns without arguing?

To respect others means . . .

- to be fair
- to take turns
- to cooperate
- to honor the rights of other people
- to recognize the importance of others
- to be courteous

- to think more highly of others than yourself
- not taking or destroying another's property
- sometimes not getting your own way
- not saying bad things about people
- not hurting others' feelings

Unit 2

Activities for Respecting Others

The activities below are a great way to teach children how to respect others.

Song

(tune: "Here We Go 'Round the Mulberry Bush")

1. This is the way we show respect,
   Show respect, show respect.
   This is the way we show respect—
   Honor the rights of others.

2. This is the way we cooperate with others . . .

3. This is the way we take turns with others . . .

4. This is the way we are courteous to others . . .

5. This is the way we are fair to others . . .

Game: Cooperation

Before class, make an extra copy of the Bible story on pages 16 and 17. (You might want to enlarge it.) Cut each line of the story into strips, or if you have a very small class, you might want to cut out larger sections of the story. Pass out all the strips to the children. Tell them that they are going to put the story back together on a table. The only rule is that they cannot speak. They may use gestures, like pointing, or shaking their heads "yes" or "no" to each other. Tell them to cooperate with each other and work as a team, but without making a sound! (*Note:* This can also be played using a Bible verse with each word written on an index card, or by having the children put a floor puzzle together.)

Craft: David Respected the King

After reading the Bible story on pages 16 and 17, make some paper crowns out of yellow tagboard. Cut one tagboard strip per child, each long enough to go around the head. Cut the top of each strip in a zigzag pattern, as shown. At a craft store, purchase fake jewels, sequins, glitter, or gold beads. Let the children decorate their crowns using the art supplies and glue, or glitter pens. When the glue dries, staple each crown so that it fits the child's head. Tell the children to tell their familiy members how David showed respect to the king.

David Respects King Saul

The first king of Israel was Saul. While he was king, he disobeyed God. God told Saul that because he had disobeyed, his kingdom would be taken away from him and given to someone else.

David was a great warrior in Saul's army. He had killed the giant named Goliath and had won many battles. A prophet told David that God had chosen him to be the next king of Israel. However, it was awhile before David actually became king.

The people of Israel loved David. They honored him as a great warrior. That made King Saul very jealous. He was so angry that he decided to kill David. When David found this out, he went into hiding. But time after time, King Saul found David and tried to kill him.

One time, Saul and his men found out that David was hiding in the desert. So they camped there. Saul was plotting again to kill David. That night, David and one of his soldiers, Abishai, went down to Saul's camp. They saw Saul asleep in the middle of the camp with all of his soldiers sleeping around him. Saul's spear was stuck in the ground near his head.

(Continued on the next page.)

Unit 2

David Respects King Saul

"Abishai said to David, 'Today God has delivered your enemy into your hands . . .'" (1 Samuel 26:8) Abishai wanted to kill Saul right then and there. But, David would not allow it.

David said, "Don't kill him! Who can lay a hand on the king that God chose and not be guilty?" David told Abishai that someday Saul would die in battle, or the Lord would take his life. David was not willing to be the one to kill the King of Israel. David told Abishai to take the spear and water jug near Saul's head. Then they left. None of the soldiers woke up because the Lord had put them into a deep sleep.

Then David climbed to the top of a hill and shouted to the commander of Saul's army, "Why didn't you guard your king? You and your men deserve to die because you did not guard your master, the Lord's anointed. Now look around you. Where are the king's spear and water jug?"

Saul recognized David's voice. He realized David could have killed him. He said to David, "I have sinned, David, my son. Come back. Because you did not hurt me today, I will not try to hurt you again. Surely I have acted like a fool."

David said, "Here is your spear. Let one of your men come get it. The Lord delivered you into my hands today, but I would not hurt you. As surely as I valued your life today, so may the Lord value my life and protect me from all trouble."

Talk About It

- Saul disobeyed God and lost his kingdom. How do you think he felt? How do you feel when you disobey God?

- Even though Saul kept trying to kill David, David would not hurt Saul. Tell about a time when someone hurt you but you didn't hurt them back.

- David respected King Saul and would not hurt him. Who do you respect? Why?

Unit 2

The Golden Rule

Name _____

One path below contains a Bible verse that teaches you how to respect others. Draw a line along the correct path.

Now copy the Bible verse correctly below.

" ___ ___ ___ ___ ___ ___ ___ ___ ___ ___ ___

___ ___ ___ ___ ___ ___ ___ ___ ___ ___

___ ___ ___ ." (Luke 6:31)

Unit 2 — Respecting Others God's Way

Name _____

God wants us to respect other people. In the puzzle below, you will find two Bible verses that tell you how to do that. Beginning with the first letter H, copy every other letter in the blanks next to the zebra. Then begin with the second letter in the puzzle, and copy every other letter in the blanks next to the monkey.

```
H A O S N W O E R H O A N V E
E A L N E O T T U H S E D R O
A G B O O O V D E T Y O O A U
L R L S P E E L O V P E L S E
```

" _ _____ _____ _____ _____ _____

_____ _____ _____ _____ _____ _____ _____ _____

__ _____ _____ _____ _____ _____ _____ _____ _____ _____ _____ ." (Romans 12:10)

"THEREFORE, __ __ ___ ___ ___ ___

OPPORTUNITY, ___ ___ ___ ___ ___ ___ ___

___ ___ ___ ___ ___ . . . "

(Galatians 6:10)

Unit 2

Poor Miss Emma!

The school cafeteria was serving chicken strips, mashed potatoes, salad, and rolls. Julie and Kelly took their trays, then stopped to get some chocolate milk to drink. They also got two little squares of butter to put on their rolls.

Every day, Julie and Kelly sat at the same table with Lexie, Holly, Kristy, and Taylor. They talked and laughed, along with everyone else in the cafeteria, until the noise got so loud that the teacher made everyone whisper.

One day, the librarian walked into the cafeteria to go through the lunch line. She always took her lunch to the teacher's lounge. She walked very slowly. She was much older than all of the other teachers. She let the children call her by her first name, Miss Emma.

As Miss Emma walked back through the cafeteria with her tray, she stepped on a pat of butter that someone had dropped. Her foot slipped, and she fell down hard, landing with her leg twisted beneath her.

All the children laughed when they saw her slip on the pat of butter. They punched each other and shouted, "Look what Miss Emma did!" They laughed and laughed. But Julie noticed that Miss Emma had a painful look on her face, and she wasn't getting up.

Julie ran over to her and asked, "Miss Emma, are you all right?"

(Continued on the next page.)

Poor Miss Emma!

"I think I broke my leg," Miss Emma said in pain. "Go get one of the other teachers, quickly." Julie saw a tear run down Miss Emma's face. She wished everyone would stop laughing. She ran to get another teacher and told her what happened. That teacher told Julie to go to the office and tell the secretary to call 911.

The cafeteria was very quiet when the ambulance drove up, and the paramedics put Miss Emma on a stretcher. They felt bad for laughing at her and making fun of her. They didn't know she was hurt.

Two weeks later, Miss Emma was back at the school library with a cast on her leg. When Julie's class came to check out books, the children all hugged her and welcomed her back. Miss Emma took Julie aside and said, "Thank you for helping me, Julie, the day that I fell. I was so embarrassed, but I was also in terrible pain. It was very grown-up of you to come to my rescue when everyone else was laughing." Then Miss Emma gave Julie a big hug.

"You're welcome, Miss Emma," Julie replied. "I'm so glad you are going to be okay."

Julie set a good example for her classmates by showing respect to the school librarian.

Talk About It

- The children were disrespectful when they laughed at Miss Emma. Tell about a time when you were disrespectful. How could you have been respectful?

- When the other children found out that Miss Emma was hurt, how do you think they felt about laughing?

- Julie showed respect to Miss Emma. Do you think Miss Emma respects Julie? Why?

- Discuss ways to show respect to your teachers, friends, and family.

Unit 2

Show Respect at Home

Name _____

Read each situation below. Then follow the instructions.

Dad is talking on the phone. If it is okay to interrupt him, write an F above number 5. If not, write an I.

The baby is taking a nap. If you should play quietly, write an R above number 6. If not, write an S.

You and your family are eating supper. If it is good manners to burp at the table, write an N above number 2. If not, write an E.

Grandma and Grandpa are visiting. If it is okay for you to leave your wet towels and dirty clothes on the bathroom floor, write an H above number 3. If not, write an F.

Someone is already watching something on TV. If you should wait your turn before turning the channel, write a B above number 1. If not, write a W.

Mom is cleaning the house. If it is okay for you to track mud in on the kitchen floor, write a C above number 4. If not, write an A.

___ ___   ___ ___ ___ ___!
1   2   3   4   5   6

Unit **2**

My Contract

Name _____

Draw a wiggly line from the big rock to all of the rocks that tell ways to respect others.

Cooperate.

Use good manners.

Steal someone's property.

Write on walls of a building.

Take turns.

Ways To Respect Others

Be fair to everyone.

Let someone else go first.

Honor people older than you.

Say bad things about someone.

Ruin someone's work.

If you want to make a commitment to honor God, copy the sentence below. Then sign your name and write the date.

I promise to do my best to respect others.

Signed _____

Date _____

On a separate sheet of paper, write 12 true things about yourself, using each letter above as a beginning letter. For example, for the letter T, you might write "tall" (if that is true about you). You may want to write a phase or a sentence. For example, using the letter H, you might say, "have blonde hair" (if that is true about you).

To tell the truth means . . .

- to be honest
- to be sincere
- to keep your word
- to say only what is true
- to have the courage to say what happened even when you might get in trouble for it
- to resist the temptation to lie
- to not deceive someone on purpose
- to not lead someone to believe what is false
- to not break your promises

Unit 3

Activities for Telling the Truth

Telling the truth can be lots of fun with the activities below and on page 26.

Game: True, Not False

Have the children put their chairs in a circle, or sit in a circle on the floor. Tell the children that they are going to take turns going around the circle. The children must take turns saying their names and then telling one true thing about themselves using the first letter of their names. For example, "My name is Jamie, and I like to jump rope," or "My name is Scott, and I like to swim." Tell the children to try to remember what every child says because when everyone is finished, you will play again. This time, however, each child must say the name of the child to his or her right and what was true about this child. Even if the player can't remember, he or she must guess. If the children remember the true thing, they stay in the game. If they say something false, they are out.

Game: Search for Truth

Label an index card with the word "TRUTH." Pick a child to go out of the room. While the child is gone, hide the card somewhere in the room. Let the player back in, and tell the child that he or she must find the TRUTH. Have the children say "hot" or "hotter" when the child is getting close to the card. They should say "cold" or "colder" if the child is moving away from the card. Tell the children that they must tell the truth in order for the player to find the card. Ask them what would happen if they did not tell the truth when saying "hot" or "cold." When the player finds the card, let another child be "it."

Song
(tune: "Twinkle, Twinkle, Little Star")

I will tell the truth each day,
Keep my word in every way.
Always honest, always true,
I won't tell a lie to you.
I will tell the truth each day,
Keep my word in every way.

Unit 3

Activities for Telling the Truth

Craft: Another Pinocchio

Ask the children what happened when Pinocchio told a lie. (His nose grew with every lie until it was very long!) Ask the children what might happen if their noses grew every time they told a lie. Would they have long noses or short noses? Ask them why it is wrong to tell lies. Discuss these concepts. Let the children think of other ways a lie could show—like growing very big ears or very big feet! Let the children use play dough and their imaginations to make dough people that have been lying. Discuss the fact that although our noses or feet don't grow when we lie, God always knows when we do. Ask the children what good things really happen when we tell the truth.

Homemade Play Dough

1 cup (240 mL) flour
1 T. (15 mL) alum
1/2 cup (120 mL) salt
1 T. (15 mL) vegetable oil
1 cup (240 mL) water
2 T. (30 mL) vanilla
food coloring (as much as needed for desired color)

Mix dry ingredients first, then add oil and water. Cook over medium heat, stirring constantly, until dough the consistency of mashed potatoes. Remove from heat. Add vanilla. Divide into balls and work in color by kneading. (Warning: This could stain your hands so use gloves when mixing. However, after thoroughly mixed, it won't stain when handled.) Store each color in an airtight container or plastic bag when not in use.

Unit
3

Ananias and Sapphira

After Jesus rose from the dead and returned to heaven, His disciples met together regularly to worship and to pray. As time went on, many people became Christians.

The church first began in the city of Jerusalem. All the believers were like one big happy family. People shared everything they had. They didn't claim any possessions were their own. There were no needy people among them. From time to time, those who owned land or houses sold them and brought the money to the disciples. Then the disciples gave it to anyone who was in need.

Ananias, and his wife, Sapphira, sold some of their land. Ananias kept back part of the money for himself, but he brought the rest to the disciples to help the needy. Ananias made it look like he was giving them all of the money that he had made from selling his property. He told a lie. Sapphira was not there when Ananias told the lie. However, she knew what Ananias was planning to do, and she went along with it.

(Continued on the next page.)

Unit **3**

Ananias and Sapphira

Peter said to him, "Ananias, how is it that the devil has so filled your heart that you have lied to the Holy Spirit? You have kept some of the money you received for the land for yourself. What made you do such a thing? You have lied not to men but to God."

When Ananias heard those words, he fell down dead! Some young men carried him out and buried him.

Later that day, Sapphira came in. She had not heard what happened. She did not know that her husband was dead. Peter asked her, "Tell me, is this the price you and your husband got for the land?" "Yes, it is," she said. She was telling the same lie that her husband had told!

Peter said, "How can you agree to test the Spirit of the Lord? Look! The men who buried your husband are at the door. They will carry you out and bury you, too."

At that moment, she fell down and died, too! Great fear came over the whole church. It was clear that God expected His followers to always tell the whole truth.

Talk About It

- If Ananias and Sapphira had told the truth about how much money they made on the sale of the land, how would this story have been different?

- Do you think we should share what we have with others? Why is it important to share with God?

- When have you told a lie and someone found out?

- How can telling lies hurt others?

Unit
3

Patchwork of Truth

Name _____

Can you tell the difference between a lie and the truth? Read all the sentences in the patchwork quilt below. If it is a true statement, color that space yellow. If it is a lie, color that space black. If you color the design correctly, you will see a quilt design.

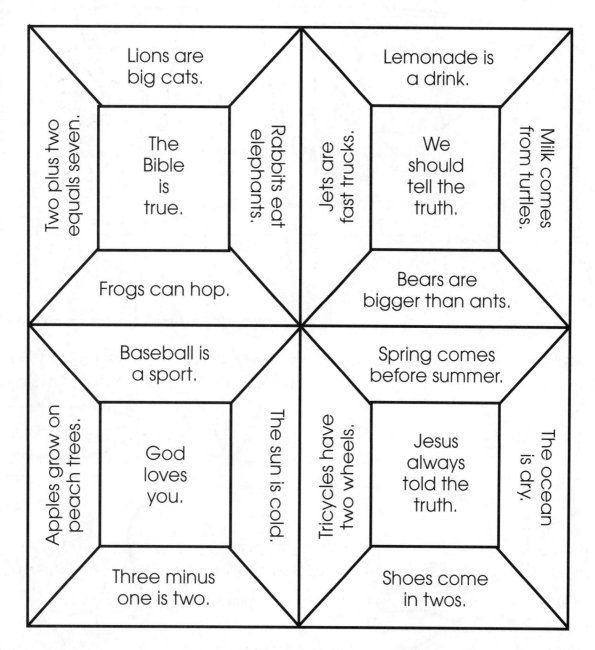

"Finally, brothers, whatever is true, whatever is noble, whatever is right, whatever is pure, whatever is lovely, whatever is admirable . . . think about such things." (Philippians 4:8)

Unit **3**

What Did Jesus Say?

Name _____

There is a phrase that Jesus said over and over again when He was talking. To find out what it was, look up the Bible verses below. Fill in the blanks with the correct words. Color the pictures.

1. "I _____ _____ _____ _____, unless you change and become like little children, you will never enter the kingdom of heaven."

(Matthew 18:3)

2. "I _____ _____ _____ _____, . . . this poor widow has put in more than all the others."

(Luke 21:3)

3. "I _____ _____ _____ _____, today you will be with me in paradise."

(Luke 23:43)

30

Unit 3

Too Many Tricks!

It was April Fools' Day, and Holly loved to play tricks on her friends. At school that day, she told Kristy that she had a spider in her hair. Kristy screamed and ran around in circles, shaking her hair wildly. Holly laughed and laughed, then she said, "April Fools'!"

When the class was outside at recess, Holly told Mike that his mother had come to pick him up. Mike went back into the classroom, but no one was there. He came back to the playground and got very angry when Holly said, "April Fools'!"

That night, Holly thought about how fun it was to play tricks on people. She decided she would keep on doing it even though April Fools' Day was over. She lay in bed, thinking of tricks to play on her friends.

Every day, Holly would say something untrue and watched what would happen. She thought it was funny that people always believed her, even when she was telling a lie. She told Lexie that Mrs. Herring had changed her mind about giving homework, so she didn't have to do it. Then Lexie got in trouble when she didn't turn in her homework. "Gotcha!" Holly laughed.

Holly even played a trick on her teacher. "Oh, no, Mrs. Herring," she said, "you must have sat down in some gum! It's stuck to the back of your dress!" Mrs. Herring tried to see the gum but couldn't find it. "I'll be right back, class," she said, as she left for the restroom. She came back into the classroom glaring at Holly who was pretending to do math problems. Holly was thinking, "Gotcha, Mrs. Herring!"

(Continued on the next page.)

Unit 3

Too Many Tricks!

One spring day, a dark thunderstorm rolled across the sky. It began to lightning and thunder. With a loud crack and pop, the lights went out. Holly was in the library, returning a catalog for Mrs. Herring. Holly smelled smoke. She looked around and saw a fire near the back of the library! "Run to the office, Holly," the librarian said. "Tell them to sound the fire alarm."

Holly did, but the principal said that without electricity, the alarm wouldn't work. He told Holly to run to her classroom and tell her teacher while he quickly told the others. Holly ran into her room and breathlessly said, "Mrs. Herring! There's a fire! We have to get out of the building."

"No, Holly," said Mrs. Herring. "I'm sure you are just going to get us all soaked in the rain and then say, 'Gotcha!'"

"No, really, Mrs. Herring! Lightning struck the building and started a fire in the library! We have to get everyone out!" Holly pleaded. Mrs. Herring decided she better check it out. She looked in the hallway and saw the other classes quickly walking out of the building. "Line up, children! Quickly!" she said, as she led them out of the room.

As the fire trucks put the fire out, Holly went to Mrs. Herring and told her she was sorry about what happened. Holly said, "I've told so many lies that now people don't believe me when I tell the truth! I won't play any more tricks, I promise. I will always tell the truth from now on."

Talk About It

- What might have happened if the teacher had ignored Holly's warning about the fire because she thought Holly was not telling the truth?

- If you tell lies often, what do people think when you tell the truth?

- Is it ever okay to lie?

Unit

3

The Lie Detector Test

Name _____

Pretend you are a police investigator giving a lie detector test. Read each story below. If the person is telling the "whole truth, and nothing but the truth," draw an arrow pointing to TRUTH. If the person is telling a lie, draw an arrow pointing to LIE.

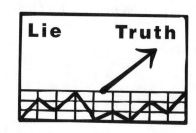

1. Brett had math and reading homework on Monday. He finished the reading homework and started to go outside to play. His mom said, "You can't go outside until you've finished your homework!" "I am finished, Mom," said Brett, as he ran out the door.

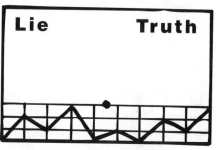

2. Travis and Jeremy were playing baseball in the yard. Jeremy pitched the ball, and Travis hit it hard. It went right through the window of Mrs. Carter's house next door! Mrs. Carter came outside and said, "Who did that?" Travis said, "I did, Mrs. Carter. I'm sorry!"

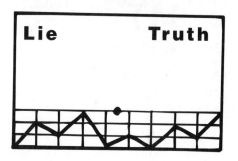

3. Justin saw a pencil on the floor near his desk. It was a Yankees' baseball pencil. "Cool!" thought Justin. He took it back to his desk to use to do his math problems. Later, he heard Robert tell Mrs. Starr that he had lost his brand new Yankees' baseball pencil that his dad had given him. "Here it is, Robert! I found it this morning," said Justin.

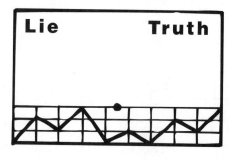

4. Emily was having a slumber party. Angie and Kristen started a pillow fight. They accidentally knocked over a lamp and broke it. Emily hid it behind the couch. The next day, Emily's mom found the lamp. She asked, "Who broke the lamp?" Emily said, "I think the cat knocked it over last night."

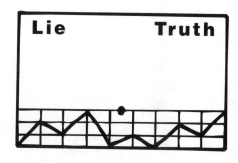

Unit
3

My Contract

Name _____

Use the letters in each cluster to spell a word. Each word starts with the letter in the middle of the cluster. Write the words in the blanks in order.

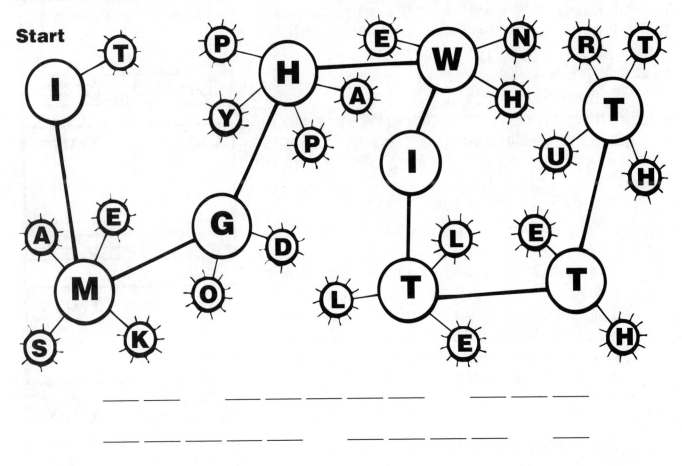

__ __ __ __ __ __ __

__ __ __ __ __ __ __

__ __ __ __ __ __ __ __ __ __ __ .

If you want to make a commitment to always tell the truth, copy the sentence below. Then sign your name and write the date.

I promise to do my best to always tell the truth.

_____

Signed _____

Date _____

Using marker or crayons color the words above. Practice self-control, so you don't color out of the lines.

To use self-control means . . .
- to behave
- to use good manners
- to do what's right without being told
- to act appropriately
- to use good judgment
- to have self-discipline

- to restrain yourself
- to act maturely
- to not depend on others to make you do right
- to not allow yourself to get out of control
- to not misbehave

Unit 4

Activities for Using Self-Control

It is fun and easy to practice self-control with the activities below and on page 37.

Game: Keep Your Eyes on Jesus

Tell the children that you are going to play a game that will take a lot of self-control. Tell them that God wants us to be self-controlled and do what is right. The best way to do that is to remember that Jesus is with us all the time and will help us to do right instead of doing wrong.

First, ask for a volunteer. Put an artist's drawing of Jesus on the wall. Tell the volunteer to keep his or her eyes on Jesus while balancing a Bible on his or her head and walking from the back of the room to the picture and touching it. (This should be fairly easy if the child takes time and concentrates.) Tell the class that it is harder to do what is right when you take your eyes off Jesus and let other things distract you.

Next, have the child start over again at the back of the room, but put a few chairs (representing hard times or temptations) in the way. Have the child also hold several things in his or her arms, like toys, books, a game, etc. (representing the cares of the world). Have the child try to balance the Bible and walk to Jesus. Let each child have a turn. Discuss the results.

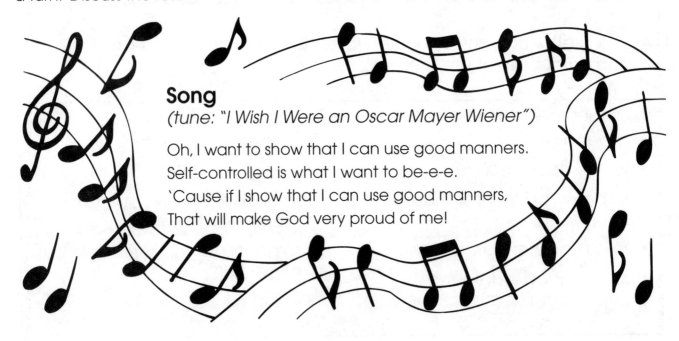

Song
(tune: "I Wish I Were an Oscar Mayer Wiener")

Oh, I want to show that I can use good manners.
Self-controlled is what I want to be-e-e.
'Cause if I show that I can use good manners,
That will make God very proud of me!

Unit 4

Activities for Using Self-Control

Craft: Bible Verse Lacing Card

Read the Bible verse on the card below. Discuss its meaning with the children in relation to self-control. Give each child a copy of the card. Tell them to color the picture and trace over the words. Have them glue their picture to a piece of tagboard or construction paper to make it sturdy enough for lacing. They should cut out their cards. Next, let the children use hole punches to make holes as indicated by the black dots. (You may want to do this ahead of time for younger children.) Then supply each child with a long piece of yarn. (A "needle" can be made by wrapping a little tape around one end of the yarn.) Tell the children to begin at the top of the card, and lace the yarn in and out of the holes, going all the way around. Then tie the two ends of yarn in a bow.

Blessed are they who... constantly do what is right. Psalm 106:3

Unit 4

Jesus Uses Self-Control

Jesus came to the earth on a mission. His mission was to save the lost so that everyone who would obey Him could go to heaven. While He was on the earth, He taught people about God and healed the sick. However, some of the Jews, especially the religious leaders, did not believe Jesus was the Son of God. His teachings made them angry. In fact, they made plans to have Him killed.

The Jewish leaders brought Jesus before the court of the Jews. There, many false witnesses came forward and lied about Jesus. But Jesus kept quiet. The high priest questioned Him some more, then declared that Jesus should die. Some men spit in Jesus' face. Other men even hit Jesus and made fun of Him. But Jesus did not lose His temper.

Then the Jews took Jesus before Pilate, the governor. Pilate asked Jesus about all the things the Jews were blaming Him for, but again Jesus kept silent. This amazed the governor. Pilate wanted to let Jesus go, but the Jews insisted that He should die. So Pilate gave into them, and then had Jesus beaten with a whip.

(Continued on the next page.)

Unit
4

Jesus Uses Self-Control

The governor's soldiers took Jesus away and gathered around Him to make fun of Him. They stripped Him and put a scarlet robe on Him, as if they believed he was a king. Then the soldiers made Jesus a crown of thorns. They knelt down in front of Jesus, pretending to worship Him. "Hail, king of the Jews," they said, but they were just making fun of Him again. Even though the people around Him were sinning, Jesus did not sin.

It got worse. The guards spit on Jesus and hit Him on the head again and again. Then they put Jesus' own clothes back on Him and led Him away to be crucified. Crucifixion was punishment for criminals, but Jesus had done nothing wrong.

Even while Jesus was on the cross, the Jewish leaders yelled mean things to Him. They said, "He saved others, but He can't save Himself! Let him come down now from the cross, and we will believe in him." But Jesus did not come down from the cross. He could have because He was the Son of God. He had the power of God. But Jesus knew that if He didn't die on the cross, then His blood could not save us. He did what God wanted Him to do, instead of getting even with the ones who were being mean to Him.

Talk About It

- When people are mean to you, what do you do?

- Jesus used great self-control when people were mean to Him. How can you use self-control when someone is mean to you?

- How can you help others to have self-control when someone is mean to them?

Unit
4

Search and Find

Name _____

In the book of Exodus, there is some good advice about how to have self-control. The words to the verse are listed out of order below. Find the words in the puzzle. Circle them. Then put the words in the correct order at the bottom of the page.

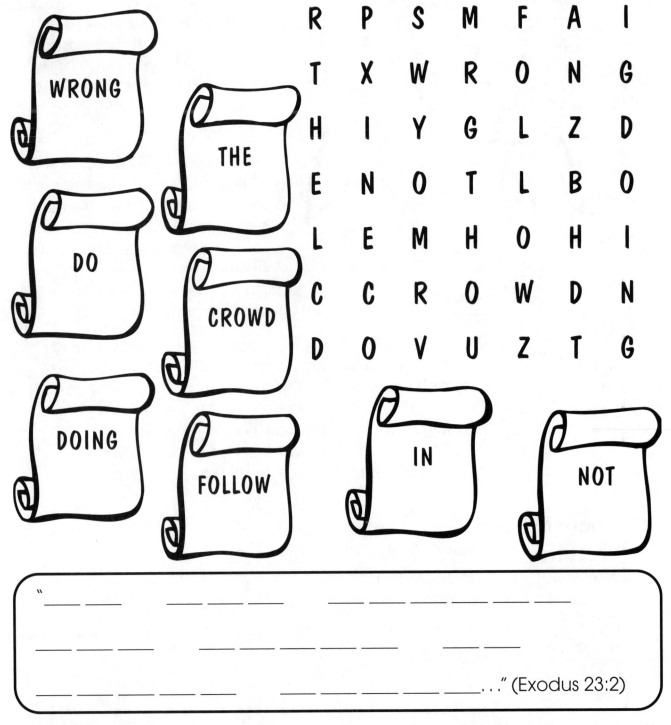

```
R  P  S  M  F  A  I
T  X  W  R  O  N  G
H  I  Y  G  L  Z  D
E  N  O  T  L  B  O
L  E  M  H  O  H  I
C  C  R  O  W  D  N
D  O  V  U  Z  T  G
```

WRONG

THE

DO

CROWD

DOING

FOLLOW

IN

NOT

" ___ ___ ___ ___ ___ ___ ___ ___ ___

___ ___ ___ ___ ___ ___ ___ ___

___ ___ ___ ___ ___ ___ ___ ___ ." (Exodus 23:2)

Unit

4

The Keys to Self-Control

Name _____

What are the keys to having self-control? The Bible gives us the answers. Look up the Bible verses below. Draw a line from the keys to the locks that tell what each verse is about.

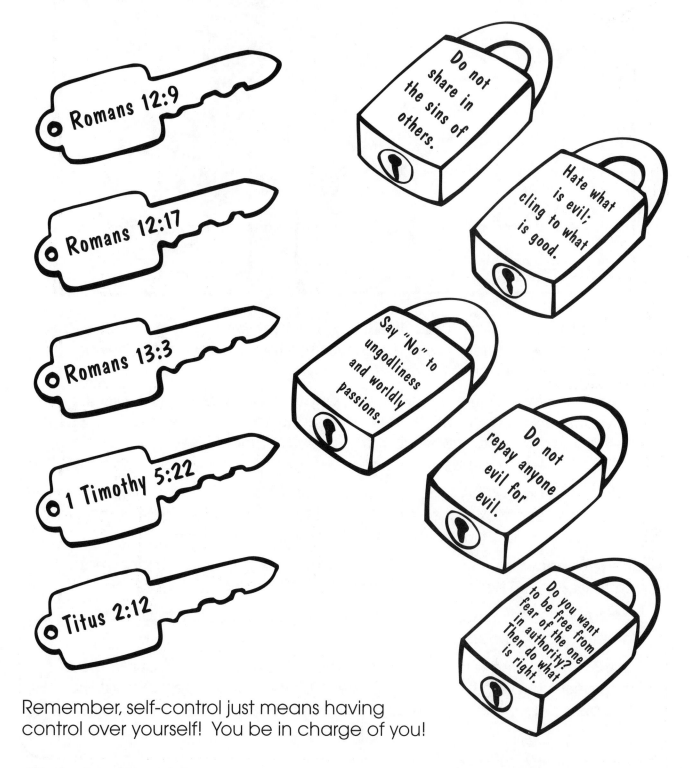

Romans 12:9

Romans 12:17

Romans 13:3

1 Timothy 5:22

Titus 2:12

Do not share in the sins of others.

Hate what is evil; cling to what is good.

Say "No" to ungodliness and worldly passions.

Do not repay anyone evil for evil.

Do you want to be free from fear of the one in authority? Then do what is right.

Remember, self-control just means having control over yourself! You be in charge of you!

Unit
4

Lack of Self-Control

Everyone was excited about the magician that was coming to Glenwood Elementary School. Before the children went to the auditorium for the show, the teacher made an announcement.

"I want all of you to be on your best behavior today during the program. Stay in your seat, and remember to keep your hands to yourselves. Don't be a talker—be a listener. And remember to use your manners," she said, as she gave the signal for them to line up.

Bailey lined up behind Max. Everyone walked in a single line to the auditorium, except Max. Whenever the teacher wasn't looking, Max ran ahead and tried to cut in line, but no one would let him.

The teacher was sitting two rows in front of Max and Bailey as the magician began to perform. "Hello, boys and girls! My name is Zombo the Great!"

"More like Dumbo the Great, if you ask me," Max said to the kids sitting around him. Bailey ignored Max and watched the show.

First, Zombo pulled a long line of colored handkerchiefs out of his sleeve, which turned into a big bouquet of flowers. Everyone clapped except Max. He was too busy pulling the ribbons off the braids of the girl sitting in front of him.

(Continued on the next page.)

Unit 4

Lack of Self-Control

Then Zombo made his assistant disappear! Max put his hands over Bailey's eyes and said, "Look Bailey! I made everything disappear, didn't I? Huh? Didn't I?" Bailey wished she could sit by someone else.

When everyone thought Zombo was going to pull a rabbit out of a hat, he surprised them by pulling out a snake instead! Max started making hissing sounds and wiggling his arm around in the air. Then he pretended that his "snake" bit everyone around him. The children were getting tired of Max's behavior. They just wanted to watch the show.

Then Zombo asked for a volunteer to come to the stage and help him. Max stood up in his chair and waved his arms wildly, yelling, "Pick me! Pick me!" Zombo chose someone else.

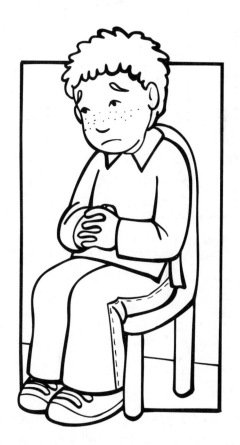

"You're a loser!" said Max, as he fell out of his chair and into the aisle. The teacher took Max by the arm and led him out of the auditorium. "It looks like you have not learned how to control yourself," the teacher said, "so you can spend the rest of the morning in the principal's office!"

Meanwhile, Bailey and the other children were having fun. They sat still, using their manners, while they watched Zombo close up a big, black box with a tiger in it. When he opened it up again, the tiger was gone, and a flock of doves flew out over the audience!

Talk About It

- Why do you think Max behaved so badly? How might things have been different if he had used self-control?

- Why do you think Zombo chose someone else to be his helper instead of Max?

- Tell about a time when you really needed self-control. How can you let Jesus help you use self-control?

Unit 4

Red Light, Green Light

Name _____

We should learn to control ourselves in every situation. Sometimes we have to tell ourselves, "No." Sometimes we should do what we know is right, even if it is hard to do. Read each situation below. If you should tell yourself to STOP, color the circle red. If you should GO ahead, color the circle green.

○ 1. The teacher is giving a math lesson. Your friend, two rows over, flies a paper airplane to you while the teacher's back is turned. You want to fly it back across the room to your friend.

○ 2. There is a rule at school that says, "Do not run in the hallways." The teacher asks you to take the attendance slip to the office. A group of kindergarten students comes out of the library. You know you should set a good example for them, so you walk.

○ 3. During worship services, your cousin passes you a note asking where your family is going for lunch. She wants you to write her back. You are hungry. You want to tell her that you hope it's Burger Land.

○ 4. You see a video game in the store that you have been wanting for a long time. You beg your mom to buy it for you. She says, "No," and you stomp your foot and yell, "You never buy me anything!"

○ 5. While you are riding your bike, a stranger calls you over to his car and offers you some candy. You know it might be a trick. You ignore him and ride home quickly.

○ 6. All the other kids at the movies throw their cups and popcorn boxes on the floor when they finish eating. You think about the person who has to clean up the mess. When the movie is over, you put your trash in the trash can.

○ 7. At church camp, a counselor brings a cooler full of canned drinks. You are hot and ask, "May I have one?" She answers, "You can have all you want!" You drink one, and then another, and then a third one. Later, you go back for another, even though your stomach is hurting.

Unit 4

My Contract

Name _____

Help the birds find their birdhouses by drawing a line from each bird to the birdhouse that completes the sentence correctly. The sentences will tell you ways to have self-control.

I will behave in . . .

I will use my . . .

rules

public

I will mind my . . .

I will do what's . . .

parents

right

I will not break the . . .

I will try not to get in . . .

trouble

manners

If you want to make a commitment to use self-control, copy the sentence below. Then sign your name and write the date.

I promise to do my best to use self-control every day.

_____

_____

Signed _____

Date _____

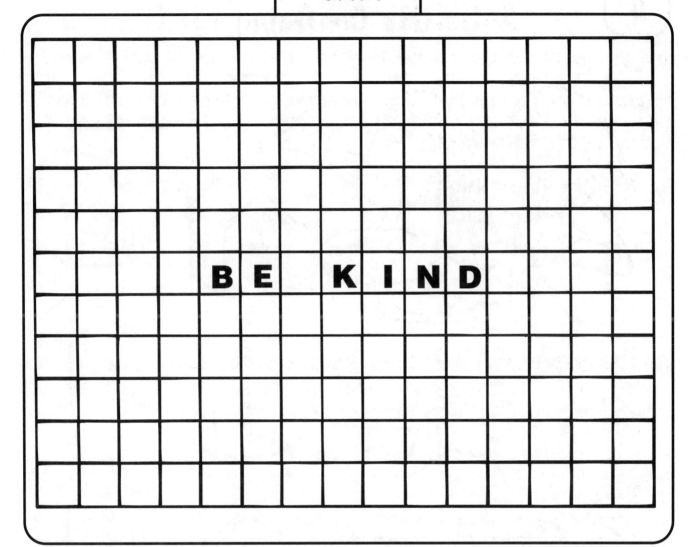

Make your own word search puzzle in the space above. Think of some people to whom you can be kind this week. Write their names in the puzzle squares. Try to use at least 6 names. Then, randomly pick letters to fill in the rest of the puzzle squares. See the example to the right.

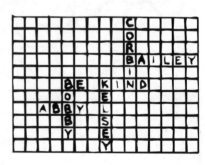

To be kind means . . .
- to care about others
- to do something nice for others
- to show compassion
- to be helpful
- to be good-hearted
- to show your love
- to treat others as you would like to be treated
- to not be cruel or mean

Unit 5

Activities for Being Kind

The activities below and on page 48 will help children learn about being kind.

Song

(tune: "Frére Jacques")

Are you being
Kind to others?
Don't delay! Start today!
Helping out and sharing,
Showing love and caring,
Every day.
Every way.

Craft and Class Project: Cheer Packages

Ask parents to send in a bag of candy and a shoebox. You can bring in some small boxes of raisins and individual bags of crackers or cookies. (Some grocers will donate items for charity.) Let each child work with a partner to decorate a shoebox. They may want to cover it with colored paper and add stickers or drawings. Put tissue paper or Easter grass in the bottom of each box, and let the children add the goodies. Have each child draw a picture of himself or herself on a piece of white paper and write on it, "My name is _____ (first name only). I am praying for you." Let the children put their pictures in the boxes they decorated. Send the boxes to a nearby hospital, perhaps to the children's ward. If possible, have some parents help you take the children to deliver the cheer packages in person and sing a Bible song. It is very beneficial for the children to see the results of their kindness!

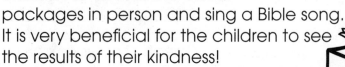

Unit

5

Activities for Being Kind

Object Lesson: Pay It Forward

Bring a couple of apples to class. Tell the children this story: *Once there was an old man who loved to eat apples. He loved things made out of apples, too, like applesauce, apple jelly, apple pie, caramel apples, and cinnamon apples. One day, the old man went outside and planted four apple trees by the side of the road. A little boy walked up to him and asked, "What are you doing?" The old man said, "I'm planting some apple trees!"* The little boy said, "But you are old, and it will take a long, long time for these trees to grow up and make apples." The old man said, "Yes, you are right. But all my life, I have enjoyed eating apples from trees that someone else planted. I don't know who they are, so I can't thank them, but I can plant some apple trees for other people to enjoy in the future. That is my way of saying 'thank you!'*

After the story, cut the apples in sections. Let each child eat one. Tell the children, "Sometimes we can show kindness to people we don't even know. This week, see if you can think of a way to show kindness to someone to pay back a kindness someone else did for you—that's paying it forward!" Discuss some ways the children can do this.

Game: Blind Dominoes

Talk to the children about being kind to handicapped people. Many times, children make fun of someone who is blind or deaf or mentally impaired. Divide the children into groups of 3 or 4. You will need a set of dominoes for each group. Let each group play a couple of rounds of War. (To play, children mix up the dominoes and then divide them equally. Next, they stack the dominoes in a long line facedown. Each child turns over a domino at the same time. Whoever has the highest number on the end of his or her domino gets all the dominoes that were played. If a tie occurs, turn over another domino, and the player with the highest number on the dominoes wins all the dominoes that were played.)

To give the children an idea of what it is like to be blind, put a blindfold on each child. Tell them they are going to play War again, but this time, with their blindfolds on. Now they will have to feel the holes in the dominoes to determine how many spots it has. When they know, they announce this number to the other players, and the other players announce theirs. Let them keep playing until you feel they are beginning to understand about being blind. Tell them to take off their blindfolds. Ask them if the game was harder to play when they couldn't see. Discuss how it must feel for a blind person to try to do everyday tasks. Discuss how other handicaps affect everyday life. Then ask the children how they can be kind to handicapped people without hurting their feelings.

Unit 5

Paul Is Shipwrecked

Paul was a missionary. He went around preaching the good news of Jesus. This made some of the Jewish leaders angry, and they had him arrested. He had to go to trial several times. Paul asked to be allowed to defend himself before Caesar, the emperor of Rome. So Paul, along with 275 other people, including some prisoners and the soldiers guarding them, set sail for Rome.

It was a very windy time of the year, and they had trouble keeping the ship on course. God told Paul what was going to happen, so Paul told the men that their voyage was going to end in disaster for them, their ship, and the cargo. But they ignored Paul's advice and sailed on.

All of a sudden, a wind as strong as a hurricane swept over them. The wind drove the ship off course, and the ship was battered by the huge waves. It was so stormy that the sun and the stars did not appear for many days. The storm raged on and on. The men gave up hope of being saved. Paul then told the men that an angel had appeared to him. The angel had told him that everyone would be saved, but the ship would be destroyed.

(Continued on the next page.)

Unit
5

Paul Is Shipwrecked

On the fourteenth day, the ship hit a sandbar and was broken to pieces by the big waves. Everyone swam to shore or floated on boards from the broken ship. They found out that they had landed on the island of Malta.

On the island, it was raining and cold. Paul and the others were wet. They had no dry clothes or blankets or food. The people who lived on the island showed them unusual kindness. They built a fire for them and made the strangers feel welcome. Then the chief official of the island, Publius, took them to his home nearby. He took care of the stranded travelers. He showed kindness to them, and they stayed there for three days.

Paul learned that Publius' father was sick in bed with a fever, so Paul prayed to God and then healed him. When the islanders heard about it, they brought other sick people to him. Paul healed them, too.

The islanders honored Paul and the other travelers in many ways during the three months they stayed on the island. When it came time for Paul and the others to sail on to Rome, the islanders brought supplies for them so that they would have all they needed to continue their trip.

Talk About It

• The people on the island were kind to Paul and the others. How can you be kind to people you don't know very well, like a new student at school, or a new family who moves next door to you?

• When was a stranger kind to you?

• How can you show kindness to someone who visits you at your home?

Unit
5

A Garden of Kindness

Name _____

Look at the pretty flowers in this garden! Each one contains a word from a Bible verse about kindness. To learn this verse, write the words from the matching flowers in the blanks. (*Note:* You may use a word more than once.)

1. "_____ _____ _____ _____

_____ _____ _____ _____."

(Proverbs 14:31)

2. "_____ _____ _____." (1 Corinthians 13:4)

3. "_____ _____ . . . _____ _____

_____." (Ephesians 4:32)

Unit
5

Some Kind Friends

Name _____

The story in Mark 2:1–12 tells how some friends showed kindness to a paralyzed man. After reading this story, color the picture below. Cut along the dashed lines to make an opening in the roof. Cut out the paralyzed man on the mat at the bottom, and attach a piece of string at each black dot. Insert the man on the mat through the opening in the roof from the back side of this sheet. Now answer these two questions:

1. How did the friends show kindness to the paralyzed man?
2. How did Jesus show kindness to him?

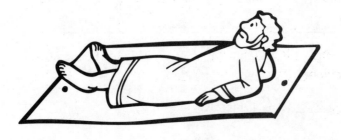

Unit 5

A Singing Surprise

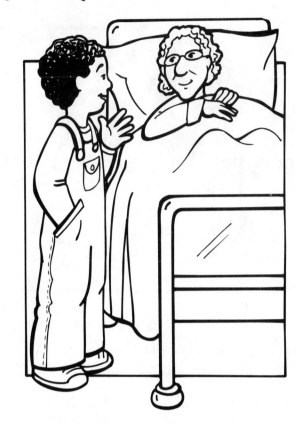

Mr. Hall, the youth minister, made an announcement to all of the first, second, and third graders. He said, "Next Saturday, meet at the church at 10 a.m. We will go to the Sunny Days Nursing Home and sing for the elderly people. Afterwards, we will go to the park for a picnic."

Dan thought to himself, "Oh, no, I don't want to go to the nursing home. I don't want to see a bunch of old people in wheelchairs and stuff. Besides, it smells funny in there. I would rather be watching cartoons on Saturday morning."

When Saturday morning came, Dan's mother woke him up at 9:15. "Better get up, Dan," she said, "so you won't be late getting to the church." Dan said, "Oh, Mom, do I have to? I don't want to spend my Saturday morning singing to old people. Besides, I want to watch cartoons."

Mom answered, "You have to learn to do kind things for other people, Dan. Watching cartoons would make you happy, but your visit will make someone else happy. It is the right thing to do."

So Dan went with the others to the nursing home. When they went inside, they found an audience in wheelchairs ready for a concert. Mr. Hall led the children in singing some hymns. Dan noticed how many of the ladies and men smiled and sang along with them.

Mr. Hall asked if anyone had a request. An elderly lady, who was known as "Nanny," asked them to sing "Amazing Grace." It was her favorite. Dan saw her tapping her fingers on her wheelchair as she sang in her high-pitched, squeaky voice. Dan realized how happy their singing had made her.

After the singing was over, Mr. Hall led the children to a room where a lady couldn't get out of bed. Dan thought how lonely she must be, never getting to go anywhere. He walked over to her bed and said, "Hi! How are you today?"

(Continued on the next page.)

Unit
5

A Singing Surprise

"Pretty good," she said with a smile. Then she asked Dan, "What is your name?" "I'm Dan," he said. "Do you have a dog at home, Dan?" Mrs. Davis asked. "Yes, I do," replied Dan, "a dachshund named Sport."

Mrs. Davis laughed and said, "Oh, a weenie dog! I love weenie dogs. You see, I used to train dogs. I owned a kennel, and people would bring their dogs to me to train them. If you check with the director, I am sure he would let you bring Sport to see me. I will show you how to teach him some tricks. Would you like that?"

"Yes, ma'am!" Dan said. "That would be cool!" Mr. Hall asked the children to sing a song for Mrs. Davis. Then they left to go to the park.

Dan had a good feeling inside. He knew he had done a kind thing by singing for the elderly people. He saw how happy it made them. But he didn't know it was going to make him happy, too! He also knew Mrs. Davis was glad that they had come to visit her, but Dan hadn't expected her to do something kind for him! A week later, Dan and Sport went to see Mrs. Davis. Sport learned two new tricks!

Talk About It

- Why is it important for us to show kindness to people like those in nursing homes and hospitals?

- Why do you think Dan was surprised that he enjoyed himself?

- Has someone ever shown you kindness that surprised you?

- How do you feel when you show someone kindness?

Unit **5**

What If It Were Jesus?

Name _____

Sometimes it is hard to be kind to very needy people or sick people. But what if Jesus were the one who was sick? Or wearing tattered clothes? It would be easy to be kind to Jesus, wouldn't it? Before you complete the rest of this page, read Matthew 25:31–40. After that, finish drawing each picture below. Then color the pictures. Next time you know that you should help someone in need, picture it this way:

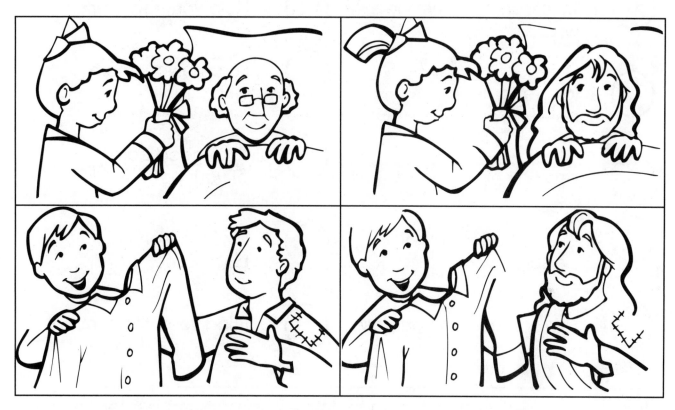

Fill in each blank with the missing letter to complete the word.

___ust picture Him

___very time someone is

___ick or needy and you will

___nderstand how to

___how kindness to others.

E   *S*

S   *J*   *U*

Now look at the letters in the blanks, going down.
Who is it?_____

Unit
5

My Contract

Name _____

Draw a smiley face in the circles next to ways
that tell how to be kind. Draw a frowny face
in the circles next to ways that do not tell
how to be kind.

○ 1. Take care of someone
who is sick.

○ 2. Ignore someone in
need.

○ 3. Lend a helping hand.

○ 4. Give a hug to a sad
person.

○ 5. Hurt someone on purpose.

○ 6. Help your teacher.

○ 7. Surprise your mom
with a gift.

○ 8. Take good care
of your pet.

○ 9. Call someone a
bad name.

○ 10. Bring your Dad the mail.

If you want to make a commitment to be kind, copy the sentence
below. Then sign your name and write the date.

I promise to do my best to be kind.

_____

_____

Signed _____

Date _____

OBEY RULES

To practice obeying the rules, follow these directions in order: Color the R red. Color all the E's blue. Color the O green. Color multi-colored stripes on the S. Color the U yellow. Color the top part of the B red and the bottom part yellow. Color purple polka-dots on the Y. Color the L your favorite color.

To obey the rules means . . .
- to follow directions
- to carry out instructions
- to do what the law says
- to respect authority
- to follow your leader
- to do what is expected of you
- to conform to a certain way of doing things
- to listen and do what you are asked to do
- to not break the rules
- to not refuse to follow instructions

Unit 6

Activities for Obeying Rules

Teaching children to obey rules is fun and easy with the activities below and on page 59.

Game: Simon Says

Tell the children that when you say, "Simon says sit down," you sit down. When you say, "Simon says stand up," they stand up. Then explain that if you don't start a command with "Simon says," they should not do it. If they do something that Simon didn't say, they are out of the game.

Game: Teacher, May I?

Have the children line up at one end of the room. Explain that when you call their name, you will tell them what to do. For example, you might tell a child to take three baby steps toward you, or one giant step, or four bunny hops. Before the child moves, however, he or she must ask, "Teacher, may I?" Then you say, "Yes, you may." If the child forgets to say, "Teacher, may I?" before moving, he or she must go back to the beginning and start over. The first child to get all the way to you wins.

Craft: Sponge Painting

Use this craft to review the Bible story on pages 60 and 61. As the children are working, ask them how Noah obeyed the rules God gave Him. To begin, give each child half of a paper plate and a wooden craft stick. Cut some clean sponges into small rectangle shapes. Bring a tube of craft paint in each of these colors: blue, green, yellow, orange, red. (Finger paints will also work well.) Squirt a little paint of each color onto several extra paper plates (not the ones cut in half). This will be their artists' palettes. Let the children use the damp sponges to dip into one color of paint

and make a curved stripe along the edge of their plate halves. Tell them to make another stripe with another color, and so on, changing sponges for each color, until they have made a rainbow. The center section underneath the rainbow should be left blank so that the children can write, "Noah obeyed God." When the paint dries, tape a wooden craft stick to the bottom of each plate, as shown.

Unit 6

Activities for Obeying Rules

Song

(tune: "I'm a Little Teapot")

I will promise to obey the rules,
When I'm home or I'm at school.
When there's someone else in charge of me,
I'll obey au-thor-i-ty.

Object Lesson: Follow the Recipe

Tell the children that you are going to make them a dessert. Give each child a copy of the recipe below. Tell them that using a recipe is like following rules. (Be sure to have the utensils on hand that you will need. Keep the ingredients in a cooler until class time, unless you have a refrigerator nearby.) Besides the ingredients listed, also have some wrong ingredients. Let the children read the recipe to you step by step. Occasionally ask the children if you can use some of the wrong ingredients you have (for example, ketchup instead of milk, etc.) Or ask if you can use only one package of cream cheese instead of two. (*Note:* Cut the recipe in half if your class is small.)

Heavenly Dirt

Ingredients:

- package of Oreo™ cookies, crushed
- large package of vanilla instant pudding
- two 8 oz. (225 g) packages of cream cheese, softened
- 2 cups (450 g) powdered sugar
- two 8 oz. (225 g) tubs of whipped topping
- 2 tsp. (10 mL) vanilla
- 3 cups (720 mL) milk

1. In a large bowl, add a large package of vanilla instant pudding to 3 cups of milk. Beat until pudding thickens.
2. Add 2 teaspoons of vanilla to the pudding.
3. Add two 8-ounce tubs of whipped topping to the pudding and mix well.
4. Now add two 8-ounce packages of softened cream cheese and 2 cups of powdered sugar to the pudding. Mix all ingredients well.
5. Pour half of the pudding into a glass bowl. Add a layer of Oreo cookie crumbs, more pudding, and top with crumbs.

Give everyone a bowl of Heavenly Dirt to enjoy!

Unit

6

Noah Obeys God

A time long ago, God saw that almost every person on the earth had become wicked. It made God sorry that He had made people. So God decided to destroy all of mankind with a great flood.

However, there was one man who was good. His name was Noah. God chose to save Noah and his family from the great flood.

God told Noah to build a huge boat, called an ark. He told Noah the exact measurements to use in building the ark and what kind of wood to use to make it. God told Noah to make lower, middle, and upper decks and to put a door in the side.

Then God told Noah to bring into the ark his wife, his three sons, and his sons' wives—eight people in all. Noah was also told to bring two of every kind of animal. Then God commanded him to take food and store it on the ark.

(Continued on the next page.)

Unit 6

Noah Obeys God

The Bible tells us that Noah did everything just as God commanded him. That means Noah obeyed God!

Then came the flood. It rained for forty days and forty nights. All the people who were disobedient to God died in the flood. Only Noah and his family were saved.

After it quit raining, it took months and months for the flood waters to go down. When the earth was finally dry, God commanded Noah to come out of the ark with his family. God also commanded him to bring the animals out of the ark. Again, Noah obeyed God.

God was pleased because Noah obeyed him. He blessed Noah and his family. God also promised that He would never destroy the whole world by a flood again. God put a rainbow in the clouds which would be the sign of His promise.

Talk About It

- What do you think would have happened if Noah had not obeyed God?

- What do you think would have happened if Noah had not obeyed God about storing food on the ark?

- Did Noah ignore God's rules? Did Noah try to change God's rules to do things his own way? Did Noah obey God's rules exactly as God commanded him to?

- What happens when you do not obey rules at school? At home?

Unit **6**

Two by Two

Name _____

God commanded Noah to build something. Then he was told to take two of every animal into it. Noah obeyed God. Connect the dots, counting by twos, to find out what Noah built.

Noah obeyed God. What else did God tell Noah to take into the ark? Draw a circle around the correct answers.

video games   his wife   a radio

food   his sons' wives   a refrigerator   his cousins

his 3 sons   a tent   an umbrella

Unit 6

Rules, Rules, Rules

Name _____

We must have rules so we can be safe. Read the rules below. Draw a line through the wrong word in each rule. Find the correct word in the cowboy's rope. Write it in the blank beside the sentence.

1. Raise your foot when you want to speak. _____

2. Don't bark while the teacher is talking. _____

3. Drivers should stop at a purple light. _____

4. Don't play ball in the igloo. _____

5. Bring your skateboard to Bible class. _____

6. Look both ways before crossing the river. _____

7. Don't talk with your ear full. _____

8. Don't pray with matches. _____

9. Paint your teeth every day. _____

10. Stand when the bus is moving. _____

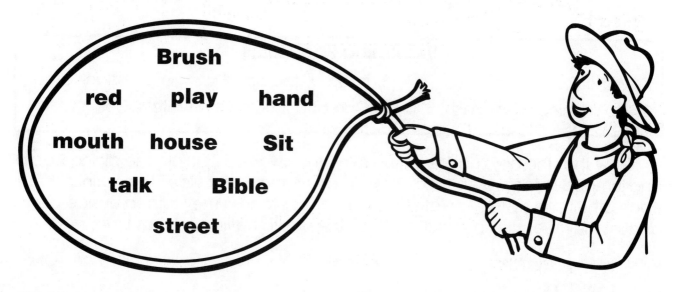

Brush

red   **play**   **hand**

mouth   **house**   **Sit**

talk   **Bible**

street

Unit

6

Pool Rules

It was finally summer time, and the city pool was open. The first day it opened was called Splash Day, and everyone got in for half price. Sam, Kenny, and Dusty were the first ones in line when the gates opened. They planned to stay all day. They ran to the diving board. All of a sudden, they heard a loud whistle. The lifeguard said, "Come here, boys. You have already broken an important rule. If you are going to swim here, you have to obey all the rules. Go to the gate, and read the rules. Then you can come back and jump off the diving board."

So the boys went to read the rules. There was a large sign by the front gate that read:

Swimming Pool Rules

1. Walk. Do not run.	3. Keep all food and drink in the snack area.
2. No pushing or shoving.	4. One at a time on the water slide.

Now that the boys had read the rules, they walked back to the diving board and jumped in the water. Next, they slid down the water slide. They dunked each other and splashed water in each other's faces. They turned upside down and let their feet stick out of the water. They were having a great time.

(Continued on the next page.)

Pool Rules

"Let's see who can do the funniest dive off the diving board," Sam said. "OK!" said Dusty and Kenny.

Dusty and Sam walked to the diving board, but Kenny wanted to go first, so he ran to the diving board. His feet slipped on the wet concrete, and he fell down. As he did, he knocked down a little girl who was standing by the pool watching people dive. The little girl fell backward and hit her head on the concrete. She cried loudly as her mother came running to check on her.

Suddenly, Kenny heard the whistle blow again. The lifeguard said, "Are you all right?" Kenny said, "Yes, I'm okay." The lifeguard said, "You broke the rule again. Now do you see why we made the rule to walk and not run on the concrete? It is to keep people from getting hurt. Now you are going to have to leave the pool for the rest of the day."

Kenny was so disappointed. He wished he hadn't broken the rule. Sam and Dusty had walked to the diving board, and they were getting to stay for the rest of the afternoon. Kenny called his mom, and he went home.

The rest of the summer Kenny remembered to always walk on the concrete at the pool. Kenny learned how important it was to obey the rules.

Talk About It

- Why did the pool have rules?

- Why was it important for everyone to follow the rules at the pool?

- Name a place you go to that has rules. What are they? Why is important to obey these rules?

- What are some of God's rules? Do you obey God's rules?

Unit
6

What Happened Next?

Name _____

When you break rules, there are consequences. Sometimes there is punishment, or sometimes you may be in danger! Read the stories below. Find the picture that shows what the consequences might be for breaking each rule. Write the letter of the correct picture in the blank beside the story.

_____ 1. Cathy's teacher told the class the rules on the first day of school. One of the rules was "No chewing gum in the classroom." One day, Cathy brought some bubble gum and chewed it during social studies class, but Mrs. Olson saw her.

_____ 2. A sign above the sidewalk at the mall said, "No skating allowed." Preston loved to skate there because the sidewalk went all the way around the mall. He began skating anyway and was soon going fast, but then he turned the corner.

_____ 3. Jeff's mom was in a hurry to get Jeff to soccer practice. She was running late. She saw that the traffic light was yellow. She sped up to hurry through the intersection. The light turned red just before she went through.

_____ 4. It is against the law to rob a bank. One day, two bad guys held up the bank. The teller quickly put the money in bags, and the bad guys tried to get away. They didn't know that someone else in the bank had called the police.

Unit
6

My Contract

Name _____

Read the words in the wagon wheels below. In the center of each wheel, write a name for the group. Also, one section was left blank in each wheel. Think of another answer for each wheel, and write it in the blank section.

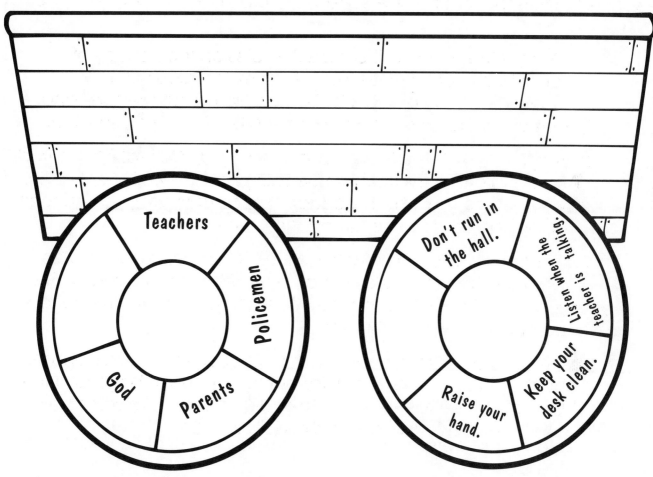

Teachers

Policemen

God

Parents

Don't run in the hall.

Listen when the teacher is talking.

Keep your desk clean.

Raise your hand.

If you want to make a commitment to obey rules, copy the sentence below. Then sign your name and write the date.

I promise to do my best to obey rules.

_____

_____

 Signed _____

Date _____

FORGIVE OTHERS

Forgiving is like erasing a mistake. In the box above, write something that someone did to you that made you mad. Say a prayer asking God to help you forgive that person. Then erase the words completely. Color the words in the box.

To forgive others means . . .

- to let go of the anger you feel when someone does wrong against you
- to treat kindly a person who has wronged you
- to try to forget about a wrong
- to overlook the faults of others
- to pardon someone

- to show mercy
- to not hold a grudge
- to not pay back evil for evil
- to not get even
- to not keep score of all the wrongs done to you

Unit 7

Activities for Forgiving Others

The activities below and on page 70 are a great way to help children learn about forgiving others.

Object Lesson: Heavy Burden

Bring in a brick for each student. (If you have time, cover each brick with paper, and write or paint the word "GRUDGE" on it.) Tell the children to think of their bricks as the angry thoughts that stay inside them when they don't forgive someone. Tell the children that when they don't forgive, they are doing something called holding a grudge. Talk about how carrying grudges around inside of you makes your heart heavy and sad. Have the children hold their bricks (their grudges) in their hands, with their arms outstretched as far as possible. See how long they can hold their bricks this way. When their arms start to droop, say, "No, keep it up there longer . . . longer . . . longer!" When they just cannot

hold their "grudges" any longer, ask them if they would like to get rid of their grudges. Ask them why. Then have them stack their bricks by the door. Tell them that forgiving someone is like taking a heavy weight off their hearts!

Object Lesson: Let It Go

Bring a helium balloon on a long string for each child. Give each child a small slip of paper. Tell the children to write down something they need to forgive someone for on their papers. Let them fold their papers in half, punch a hole in them, and then tie them to their balloon strings. Talk to the children about not holding grudges. Tell them that it is healthy for them to let go of their anger and not hold it in. Tell them that God is pleased when we forgive, just like He forgives us. Then lead the children outside. Tell them that when you give the signal, they are to let go of their balloons and their anger at the same time. Tell them that as they let go of their balloons, everyone will say, "I forgive you!"

Unit **7**

Activities for Forgiving Others

Song

(tune: "Ten Little Indians")

Jesus loves me and forgives me.
Jesus loves me and forgives me.
Jesus loves me and forgives me.
I'll forgive like Jesus.

I'll forgive. I won't hold grudges.
I'll forgive. I won't hold grudges.
I'll forgive. I won't hold grudges.
I'll forgive like Jesus.

Game: Paper Walk

Lay pieces of construction paper in a big circle like stepping stones around the edge of your room. Put as many papers down as you can, with a little space between each one. Designate one "stone" as START. Have the children line up at the starting stone. Each child takes a turn rolling a die. The first player takes the number of steps rolled and stands there. The next player does the same, and so on. However, anytime a player lands on a space that is already occupied, this new player takes that player's place, saying, "I'm sorry!" The player that is being removed says, "I forgive you," and goes back to the beginning. This will be hard for some children who are especially competitive, but it will reinforce the habit of verbally forgiving others. The first child all the way around the room wins.

Craft: The Cross

Tell the children that this craft will remind them that Jesus died on the cross to forgive us of our sins. He is our example that we should forgive others. Give each child two wooden craft sticks and a long piece of yarn or string. Tell them to place one stick over the other to make a cross. Then they wind the string around the intersection of the sticks, in an X shape. Make sure they leave a few inches of string hanging when they start, so they can tie it to the end of the string when they finish wrapping it around the sticks. You may want to provide a fine-tip marker they can use to write "Jesus forgives" on their crosses.

A Father Forgives

Jesus was an excellent storyteller. He often taught important lessons by telling parables. A parable is an earthly story with a heavenly meaning. One parable Jesus told teaches about forgiveness.

Once upon a time, a man had two sons. The younger one told his father he wanted his inheritance money right away. So the father gave him his share of the money.

Then the son moved away and spent all of his money doing wild and sinful things. About the same time that he ran out of money, there was a severe famine in the land. The young man was poor and hungry, so he got a job feeding pigs. He wished he could at least have as much food as the pigs, but no one gave him anything.

When he came to his senses, the son remembered that the servants at his father's house had plenty to eat. He decided to go back home and tell his father that he had sinned. He would say that he was not worthy to be called his son, but he would like to become one of his father's hired servants. So he set out for home.

(Continued on the next page.)

Unit 7

A Father Forgives

While he was still a long way off, his father saw him and was filled with love for him. His father didn't wait for him to get there. He ran to meet him! He threw his arms around him and kissed him.

The son said, "Father, I have sinned. I am not good enough to be called your son." But the father interrupted him and told the servants to bring the best robe and put it on him. He told them to put a ring on his finger and sandals on his feet. He also told the servants to prepare a feast so that they could celebrate his son coming home.

The older son heard that his brother had come back home. He got very angry and refused to go to the feast. His father came out and pleaded with him to come in, but he wouldn't. He said, "All these years I have worked hard for you. I have never disobeyed your orders. Yet you have never given me a party so I could celebrate with my friends." The son was angry because his younger brother had spent all of his inheritance doing wild and sinful things, and now his father was throwing a party for him!

The father answered, "My son, you are always with me. Everything that I have is yours. But we must celebrate and be happy, because this brother of yours was dead and is alive again; he was lost and now is found."

Talk About It

- Do you think the father should have forgiven his youngest son?
- Do you think the older son should have forgiven his brother?
- When have you forgiven someone when it was really hard?
- How did you feel when someone forgave you for something?

72

Unit 7

Why Should I Forgive?

Name _____

The Bible tells us that there is a very important reason why we should forgive others. That reason is written below. To find the missing words, put all the words in the Word Box in alphabetical order. First, write them in the numbered blanks in the ABC Order box. Then copy them in the blanks that have the same number. Some answers are used more than once.

"For _____ _____
      5   9

_____ _____
   3   6

_____ they sin _____
  8   1

_____ , your _____
  9   4

Father will also _____
                     3

_____ . But _____ _____ _____ not
  9   5   9   2

_____ _____ their
   3   6

_____ , your Father will not
  7

_____ your _____ ."
   3   7

(Matthew 6:14–15)

Word Box	ABC Order
if	1. _____
when	2. _____
heavenly	3. _____
do	4. _____
forgive	5. _____
men	6. _____
against	7. _____
sins	8. _____
you	9. _____

Unit
7

What Is Forgiveness?

Name _____

The Bible makes it clear that we should forgive others. What is forgiveness all about? Find out by filling in the missing letters below. In each blank, write the beginning letter of the picture that is below the blank.

Unit
7

Live and Learn

It was Kelly's turn to dry the dishes and put them away. She got a clean kitchen towel and dried the plates and the glasses. She picked up her mom's antique, rose-colored crystal bowl to dry it. It was slippery, and she accidentally dropped it. It broke into dozens of little pieces!

"I'm sorry, Mom! I didn't mean to!" Kelly cried. She was afraid her mom would get mad. Would she be punished?

"Step back, Kelly," Mom said, "so you won't cut your feet on the glass." Mom swept up the glass, and Kelly saw tears in her eyes. Oh, no, now she was really going to be in trouble.

"Don't cry, Mom," said Kelly. "I'll save up my money and buy you another one."

"You can't," Mom said. "That was an antique bowl that my great-grandmother gave me. You can't buy these in the stores anymore. That's why I'm crying. But I learned a long time ago, Kelly, that people are more important than things. This bowl was not what I loved. I loved my great-grandmother, and nothing can destroy the wonderful memories I have of her. Besides that, you are more important than an antique bowl. I know it was an accident. I forgive you."

"Thank you, Mom," Kelly said, relieved. She hugged her mom and finished drying the dishes.

(Continued on the next page.)

Unit 7

Live and Learn

Later that day, Kelly was working on a 100-piece puzzle in her room. She only had about 10 more pieces to put together, and then the puzzle would be finished.

Just then, Kelly's three-year-old sister walked into her room. She stood on her tiptoes to see what Kelly was doing. She accidentally pulled the table over. The puzzle went crashing to the floor, all over the carpet.

"Look what you did, Trisha!" yelled Kelly. "I was almost finished with that puzzle, and now you've ruined it! I'm so mad at you! I'm going to tell Mom!" Kelly pushed Trisha down and yelled, "MOM!"

As Mom walked in the door, Kelly griped, "Mom, look what she did! She ruined my puzzle. Now I'll have to start all over again. Make her get out of my room and stay out!"

Mom looked at Kelly and said, "How would you have felt, Kelly, if I had treated you that way this morning when you broke my antique bowl? You didn't mean to do it, and I forgave you. Your sister didn't mean to pull the table over. She's little. It was an accident. Now what do you need to do?"

Kelly thought for a minute. Then she hugged Trisha. "I forgive you," she said. She picked up the pieces that were still stuck together and put them back on the table. Trisha put the other pieces back in the box. "Tomorrow, I'll start over," Kelly said with a smile, "but I think I will lock the door first!"

Talk About It

- Do you think Kelly's mom should have forgiven her?

- Why did you think it was hard for Kelly to forgive her little sister?

- When was it hard for you to forgive someone?

- When did you really want to be forgiven? Were you forgiven?

- Is it true that people are more important than things? Why?

Unit 7

God Forgives, We Forgive

Name _____

Psalms 51:1 says, "*Have mercy on me, O God, according to your unfailing love; according to your great compassion blot out my transgressions.*" Transgressions are sins. Use "White Out" or "Liquid Paper" to blot out the sins from the person in the first box. That's what it's like when God forgives you.

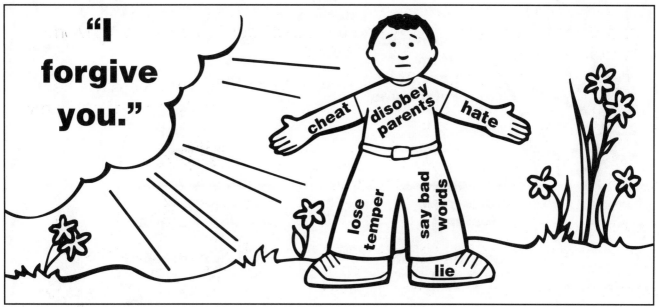

Now blot out the grudge that is in the heart of the child in this picture. This is how you should forgive! Matthew 18:35 says, "*. . . forgive your brother from your heart.*"

Unit **7**

My Contract

Name _____

When is it time to forgive others? Draw hands on the clock, pointing only to each correct answer. This will be a funny-looking clock with lots of hands!

when a person says, "I'm sorry"

when you think of how God forgives you

never— just get even

often

as often as they ask

when someone hurts your feelings

when you realize you have been holding a grudge

only between 10:00 and 12:00

when someone makes you mad

only when I feel like it

only in the summer

even when they don't ask for it

If you want to make a commitment to forgive others, copy the sentence below. Then sign your name and write the date.

I promise to do my best to forgive others.

_____

_____

Signed _____

Date _____

BEE

_____

R e e s p o n s i b l

_____

Both of the words above are spelled incorrectly. Use a red crayon or marker to cross out the misspelled words. Then write the two words, spelled correctly, on the blank lines.

To be responsible means . . .
- to be reliable
- to be trustworthy
- to show people they can depend on you
- to do what you are supposed to do
- to do a job well

- to be someone who can be counted on
- to complete a task in the correct way
- to take care of property
- to keep promises
- to do your duty

Unit **8**

Activities for Being Responsible

Children can practice being responsible by doing the activities below.

Game: Job Charades

Ahead of time, write down a list of occupations on a piece of paper (for example: doctor, teacher, car mechanic, secretary, grocery store checker, farmer, pilot, soldier, mail carrier, dentist, construction worker, zookeeper, etc.). Make sure there is one per child. Cut the list into strips, and put them in a cup. Have the children take turns drawing out a strip and acting out the job. Tell them to act out the responsibilities that someone with that job would have. The others can guess what kind of worker is being acted out.

Song
(tune: "The Farmer in the Dell")

Depend on me to do,
The things I promised to.
I can be responsible
And trustworthy, too.

Craft: Responsibility Mural

You will need a roll of butcher paper or newsprint. Sometimes newspaper offices will donate partial rolls of newsprint, or rolls of paper can be bought at teacher supply stores. Roll out the paper the length of your room. Move tables and chairs back so the children can sit or lie on the floor while coloring. Tell the children that today they are going to make a mural—a long continuous drawing. Ask if any of them have ever seen a mural. Explain that they will be making a responsibility mural. Tell

the children to think about some responsibility they have at home (for example: feeding the dog, setting the table, taking out the trash). Assign each child a section of the paper, and draw lines between the sections. Then have the children draw their responsibilities on the paper. Emphasize that the children should make their pictures big enough to go from the top of the paper to the bottom of the paper in their section of the mural. When the children finish, display the mural with a sign that says, "We Are Responsible." Let the children sign the section they created.

Unit

8

Joseph Is Responsible

Jacob had many sons, but he loved Joseph best of all. Jacob gave Joseph a beautiful coat of many colors. This made his brothers mad. Joseph also had dreams about his brothers bowing down to him. This made his brothers mad, too. One day, Jacob sent Joseph to go to the fields where his brothers were tending the sheep. He told Joseph to see how they were doing and then come back and report to him.

When Joseph found his brothers, they were mean to him. They sold Joseph as a slave to a caravan of merchants. Later, the merchants sold him to a man named Potiphar in the country of Egypt.

Potiphar was one of Pharaoh's officials. (Pharaoh was the king of Egypt.) Joseph worked hard and was very responsible while he served in Potiphar's house. So Potiphar put Joseph in charge of his household. He trusted Joseph with everything that was his. However, Potiphar's wife told a lie about Joseph. Potiphar believed her and had Joseph put in prison.

Even while Joseph was in prison, he acted in a responsible way. The guard put Joseph in charge of all the other prisoners. He also made Joseph responsible for all that was done there because he knew Joseph would be responsible and do what he was told. The Lord was pleased with Joseph. He blessed him in all that he did.

(Continued on the next page.)

Joseph Is Responsible

God gave Joseph the ability to interpret dreams. Later, Joseph was asked to interpret a dream for Pharaoh. The dream was a warning that there would be seven years of plenty; then there would be seven years of famine when food would become scarce. Joseph told Pharaoh to plan ahead and store up huge amounts of food.

This idea pleased Pharaoh. He told Joseph, "You will be in charge of my palace. All of my people will obey your orders. Only because I am king will I be greater than you. I hereby put you in charge of all of Egypt." During the seven years of plenty, Joseph carried out the job of storing grain. There was so much grain and food that it could not be counted.

When the famine came, Joseph was responsible for opening the storehouses and selling grain to the people. Eventually, Joseph's own brothers came to buy food because the famine was severe in their land, too. They didn't recognize Joseph at first, and Joseph was kind to them. Later he told them that he was their brother whom they had sold into slavery. Joseph forgave his brothers and provided food for them and their families. Joseph realized that it was God's plan that had sent him to Egypt to store food so that his family could be saved from the famine!

Talk About It

- Joseph was responsible in every thing he did. Did good things come from him being responsible?

- What happens when you are responsible? What are some of your responsibilities?

- What happens when you are not responsible?

- How can you be responsible at home? At school? At church?

Unit **8**

God Blessed Joseph

Name _____

God was with Joseph throughout his whole life. In every situation, Joseph did the very best job he could do. You will find the answers below are incomplete sentences about the story of Joseph. Write your answers in the boxes, going down. Be sure the number of the question matches the number where you put your answer. When you are finished, a very special word will appear in the gray box.

1. God helped Joseph interpret Pharaoh's _____.

2. Joseph forgave his _____.

3. The guard put Joseph in charge of all the other _____.

4. Joseph realized it was God's _____ that had sent him to Egypt to save his family.

5. Joseph interpreted this king's dream.

6. It was Joseph's responsibility to store up _____ before the famine.

7. Jacob sent Joseph to check on his brothers who were tending the _____.

8. Name of Pharaoh's official whom Joseph worked for

9. Even while in prison, Joseph acted in a _____ way.

10. Potiphar's _____ told a lie about Joseph.

11. Joseph's brothers sold him as a _____ to a caravan of merchants.

12. Pharaoh's dream meant that there would be 7 years of _____ (shortage).

13. First, there would be seven years of _____ (more than enough).

14. Pharaoh put Joseph in charge of the whole land of _____.

Unit

8

Work and Play

Name _____

Gary and Joe want to go to the lake to swim and have a picnic. Their mom and dad said they would take them if they finished all their chores. Help Gary and Joe get their chores done by drawing two lines through the maze to the lake. But don't let them get sidetracked. That would be irresponsible!

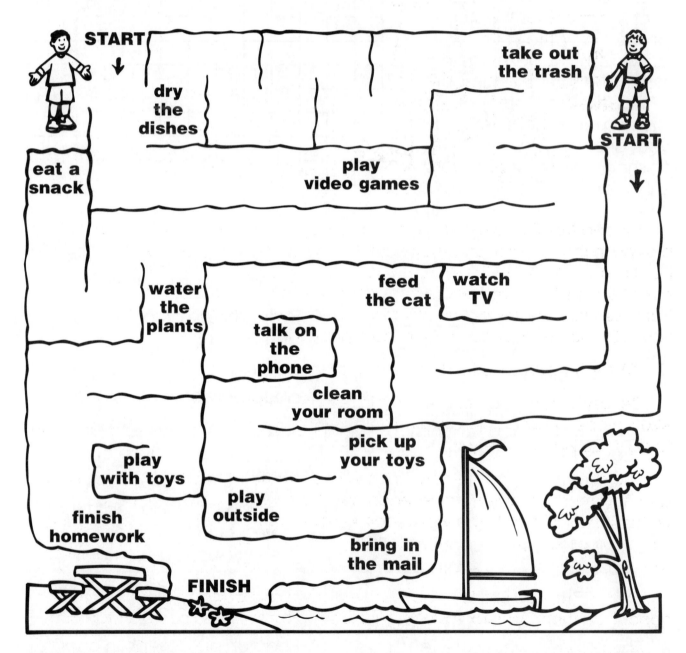

"Whatever you do, work at it with all your heart, as working for the Lord, not for men." (Colossians 3:23)

84 ©Teacher Created Materials, Inc.

Unit
8

A Good Job

Mr. and Mrs. Cox lived next door to Berkley. One day, the Coxes saw Berkley playing in the sprinkler, and they called her to come to the fence. They asked her if she would like to have a job. "We are going on vacation for two weeks," Mrs. Cox said, "and we need a responsible person to take care of our dog, Patches, while we are gone. Would you be interested in the job? We will pay you $20 when we get back, if you do a good job."

"Wow! I would love to! Let me ask my mom if it's okay," Berkley said.

Berkley's mom told her it was a big responsibility to take care of someone else's property, especially a dog. She asked Berkley if she was sure she wanted to do it. Berkley was very sure!

The day before they left, Mr. Cox showed Berkley where the food was kept and how much to give Patches each day. He said, "Be sure he has enough water since it is so hot. The way a dog keeps cool in the summer is by drinking lots of water, so that is very important. You will also need to use this leash and take him for a walk two or three times each week. Can you handle that?"

"Yes, sir," replied Berkley. She reached down and patted Patches on the head. "Ok, then," Mr. Cox said, "we are leaving tonight. You can start tomorrow."

(Continued on the next page.)

Unit
8

A Good Job

The next day, Berkley felt important as she did her job. Every day for a week and a half, Berkley fed and watered Patches.

Just three days before the Coxes were supposed to come back home, something terrible happened! Just as she opened the gate, Patches took off running—out the gate and down the street! "Patches! Come back here!" shouted Berkley.

Berkley ran down the street chasing Patches, thinking, "Oh, no, what will Mr. and Mrs. Cox say if something happens to Patches! What if he gets away and I can't find him? It's my job to take care of him!" Berkley ran and ran, calling, "Patches! Patches!"

Patches saw a cat in Miss Cameron's yard. He chased it around and around the yard until it climbed high up in a tree. Berkley had almost caught up with Patches, when he took off again. He ran through flower beds, over a big rock, and under a parked car.

Then Patches finally stopped . . . right in a big mud puddle! When Berkley caught him, he was covered from head to toe in brown mud.

Berkley carried him home, bathed him, and dried him off. He looked as good as new, but now Berkley was dirty all over.

On Saturday, when the Coxes came home, they were so glad to see Patches. They called Berkley to come over and get her money. Mrs. Cox said, "You must have done a great job with Patches! He looks clean and healthy and happy! Thank you, Berkley. I hope he was no trouble."

"Oh, no," giggled Berkley, "no trouble at all."

Talk About It

- What did Berkley do that was responsible? What did she do that was *super* responsible?

- What might have happened if Berkley hadn't been responsible?

- What is an important responsibility you have? What could happen if you aren't responsible?

Unit

8

What If?

Name _____

Being responsible means doing your job well. How would the world be different if people didn't do their jobs well? What if everyone was irresponsible? Read each "what if" question below. Think about it. Discuss what could happen if these people were irresponsible! Then, choose one of the "What if's" and illustrate it on the back of this paper.

1. What if a doctor prescribed the wrong medicine?

2. What if a teacher never taught reading?

3. What if a babysitter was watching TV while the baby crawled out the front door?

4. What if a pilot fell asleep while flying a plane?

5. What if an ambulance driver forgot to put gas in the ambulance?

6. What if a gardener never watered his flowers?

7. What if a preacher slept till noon on Sunday?

8. What if a mail carrier lost a box of letters?

9. What if it was your job to take out the trash, but you never did?

10. What if it was your job to feed the fish, but you never did?

Unit

8

My Contract

Name _____

Help the astronauts get to the right planets. Draw a line from the space shuttle only to the planets that tell ways that you can be responsible.

If you want to make a commitment to be responsible, copy the sentence below. Then sign your name and write the date.

I promise to do my best to be responsible.

_____

_____

Signed _____

Date _____

Tape a piece of black construction paper to the back of this page. Use a straight pin to punch holes in every little dot in the words and design above. This takes patience! When you are finished, remove the tape. Hold the black page up to the light or display it in a window. Can you read the message?

To be patient means . . .
- to wait without complaining
- to endure hardship with self-control
- to hold on for a while
- to stick it out
- to handle trouble without getting upset
- to be tolerant of other people's ways
- to remain calm during a delay
- not losing your temper
- not getting angry in a stressful situation

Unit 9

Activities for Being Patient

The activity below provides an exciting way for the children to learn about being patient.

Game: Pyramid Patience

You will need a package of fifty Styrofoam™ cups for each group of children. (For younger children, you may want to use fewer cups.) Make sure each group has enough space on the table or floor so that it does not interfere with the other groups. Tell the children that they are going to work together with their group to build a pyramid out of cups. They should stack the cups higher and higher until they have used every cup. Tell the children that they will have to be patient with each other as they take turns and work together. They will also have to be patient if the cups fall and they have to start over, or if they have some cups left over and have to rebuild the pyramid in order to use all the cups. Anyone who gets impatient with others in the group is out of the game. The first team to build a pyramid using all the cups wins.

Song

(tune: *"The Farmer in the Dell"*)
Be patient while you wait.
Be patient while you wait.
Don't lose your temper or complain.
Be patient while you wait.
(Sing it again, pausing a few seconds
each time before singing "wait.")

Object Lesson: The Patience of a Farmer

Talk to the children about how we get our vegetables. Explain that a farmer plants the seeds. Then he or she waits patiently for the sun and rain to make them to grow. Weeks later, the farmer harvests the vegetables, boxes them up, and sends them to the stores for us to buy. To get an idea of how farmers have to be patient while their crops are growing, let each child plant three, dried pinto beans in a Styrofoam™ cup filled with potting soil. Place the beans where they can get some sunlight. Water the plants when the soil gets dry. Each time the children come to class, let them see how much their plants have grown. It takes patience to wait for good things to grow!

Abraham Waits Patiently

One day, the Lord said to Abraham, "Leave your country, your people, and your home. Go to a special place I will show you. I will make you into a great nation. I will bless you."

Abraham was already 75 years old when God made that promise to him. He didn't understand how God could make his family be so big that it became a great nation of people when he had no children. It seemed like a promise that couldn't come true, but Abraham had faith in God. He believed that God would make the promise come true.

So Abraham and his wife, Sarah, went to live in the land of Canaan. While he was living there, God spoke to him again. God told Abraham that he would some day have a son. He also told him again that a great nation would come from his family. He would have so many descendants that they could not be counted, just like there are so many stars in the sky that they cannot be counted!

Abraham waited and waited. He was getting very old—too old to become the father of a little baby. But Abraham was patient. He knew in time, God would keep His promise.

(Continued on the next page.)

Unit 9

Abraham Waits Patiently

When Abraham was 99 years old, God told Abraham that the next year, he would have a son. By then, he would be 100 years old! And his wife, Sarah, would be 90!

But it happened just as God had promised that it would! Abraham and Sarah had a little baby boy. They named him Isaac.

Isaac grew up and had two sons named Jacob and Esau. They were Abraham's grandchildren. Jacob grew up and had twelve sons and one daughter. They were Abraham's great-grandchildren. Those children grew up and had sons and daughters. Abraham's family grew and grew through the years until later on, there were so many of them that they could not be counted. They were as numerous as the stars in the sky!

God first made the promise to Abraham when Abraham was 75 years old. He was 100 when the promise came true! Abraham waited patiently for 25 whole years!

Talk About It

- Could you wait for 25 years for a promise to come true?

- Sometimes we need patience when we are learning something new. What have you needed patience to learn?

- What happens when you are not patient at home? At school? With your friends?

Unit **9**

Be Patient With People

Name _____

Sometimes being patient means waiting for something. But being patient can also mean keeping your cool when someone is getting on your nerves. Maybe a small child is screaming and crying at the table next to you in a restaurant. You have to be patient. Maybe someone at school keeps bugging you. Instead of losing your temper, you must be patient with that person. God wants us to be patient with other people. To learn a Bible verse about patience, use the clocks and the written times to help you figure out which vowel to write in each blank.

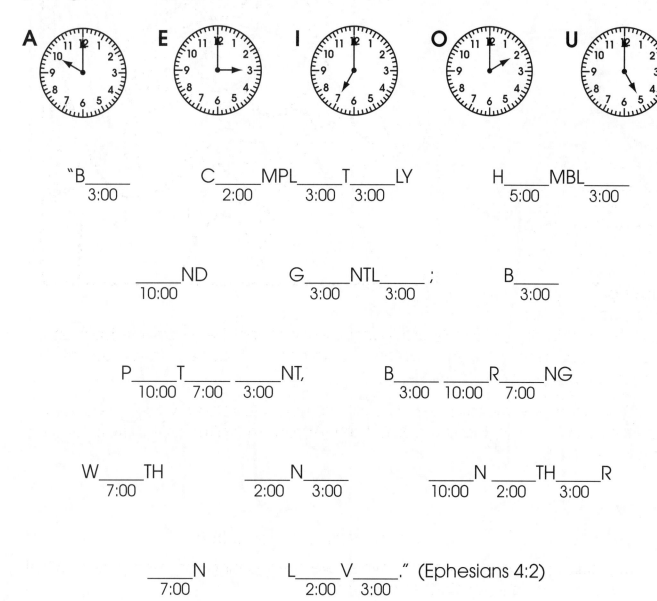

"B____   C____MPL____T____LY   H____MBL____
3:00   2:00   3:00   3:00   5:00   3:00

____ND   G____NTL____ ;   B____
10:00   3:00   3:00   3:00

P____T____ ____NT,   B____ ____R____NG
10:00 7:00   3:00   3:00 10:00   7:00

W____TH   ____N____   ____N ____TH____R
7:00   2:00 3:00   10:00 2:00   3:00

____N   L____V____." (Ephesians 4:2)
7:00   2:00 3:00

Unit 9

Patience of a Farmer

Name _____

James 5:7, 8 says, "*Be patient, then, brothers, until the Lord's coming. See how the farmer waits for the land to yield its valuable crop and how patient he is for the autumn and spring rains. You too, be patient.*" Look at the first picture of the patient farmer. Then look at the second picture and find 8 things that are different. Circle them. Then color the pictures.

Unit 9

Waiting for Something Great

"I have a surprise to tell you about," Dad told Sam and Mom. "One week from today, we are going on a vacation to DizzyWorld!"

"You're kidding!" Sam said, as he ran to hug his dad. "Thank you! Thank you! Thank you! I have wanted to go there for three years! Finally, we get to go! Yippee!" Dad grinned as he watched Sam jump up and down.

"You may ask Dusty to go with you so you will have someone your age to go on the rides with," Dad added.

"Yea! I'm going to call him right now!" Sam said.

The next day, Sam was miserable. "What's wrong?" asked his mom. Sam said, "It's six whole days till we get to go to DizzyWorld. I can't wait. It seems like that day will never get here."

Mom said, "When you have to wait, make it easier on yourself by playing the Waiting Game. Think about what you can do between now and then to make the time go faster."

Sam said, "Well, I could . . . let's see . . . I could set up a lemonade stand down on the corner each day and make some spending money for the trip. Maybe Dusty will help me."

"Good idea!" said Mom, and she went to make a big pitcher of lemonade.

(Continued on the next page.)

Unit **9**

Waiting for Something Great

Finally, the day came for the big trip. They had only ridden in the car for 30 minutes when Sam said, "How much longer till we get to DizzyWorld, Mom? It's boring to ride in the car. I'd rather be riding on the roller coaster!"

"Oh, it's two more hours until we get to DizzyWorld. Maybe you boys should play the Waiting Game," Mom suggested.

So the boys thought about what they could do to pass the time until they got there. First, they played the Animal Game. They named all the animals that started with an A until someone couldn't think of one. That meant the other person won. Then they played again with B words, and so on.

Later on, they played the Sign Game. They took turns finding words on signs that begin with the letters A to Z. They were having fun when all of a sudden, Dad said, "Look! There's DizzyWorld!"

Sam and Dusty were so excited. They could hardly wait to ride Rocket Mountain Roller Coaster. After they parked, a shuttle bus picked them up in the parking lot and took them to the entrance. They couldn't believe what they saw there. It was a long, long line of gray-haired adults.

"Oh, no! Look at that long line!" said Dusty. Sam shrugged his shoulders and said, "Well, it looks like we will have to play the Waiting Game again just to get into the park!" It was a good thing that Sam and Dusty learned how to wait patiently because they had come to DizzyWorld on Senior Citizens Get-in-Free Day!

Talk About It

- Why was it hard for Sam to be patient until it was time to go on the trip?

- Is it hard for you to be patient when you are waiting for something special? Why?

- What are some things you do when you are trying to be patient?

- How are things more difficult when people are impatient?

I Can Be Patient

Name _____

Having patience makes it possible to use your time wisely while you are waiting. List some things you could do while you are waiting in each of the situations below.

If you had to wait a long time in the waiting room at the doctor's office, some things you could do while waiting are . . .

_____
_____
_____

If you were very hungry, and Mom was cooking dinner, some things you could do while waiting are . . .

_____
_____

If you were standing in a long line waiting for a ride on a roller coaster, some things you could do while waiting are . . .

_____
_____
_____

If you were planning to swing on the playground at recess, but all the swings were taken when you got there, some things you could do while waiting are . . .

_____
_____

My Contract

Name _____

It takes a lot of patience to catch a fish. Help this boy catch some! Draw his fishing line from fish to fish, connecting only the ones that tell how to have patience. Don't catch the others!

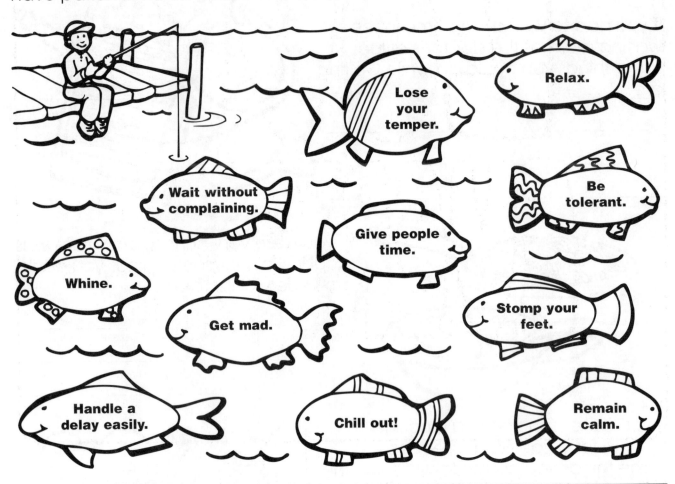

If you want to make a commitment to have more patience, copy the sentence below. Then sign your name and write the date.

I promise to do my best to have more patience.

_____

_____

Signed _____

Date _____

LOVE EVERYONE

Make a border around the words above by writing the names of people you love.

To love everyone means . . .

- to show others you care
- to be kind to people who are different from you
- to get along well with others
- to be friendly
- to want good, not bad, for other people

- to be fond of people
- to care about people
- to not hate anyone
- to not mistreat anyone

Unit 10

Activities for Loving Everyone

The activities below and on page 101 are a great way to encourage children to share their love with others.

Song

(tune: "He's Got the Whole World in His Hands")

Chorus:

I love the whole world, everyone.
I love the whole world, everyone.
I love the whole world, everyone.
I love the whole world, everyone.

Verses

1. I love the girls and the boys, everyone…
2. I love the rich and the poor, everyone…
3. I love the young and the old, everyone…
4. No matter what color skin, everyone…

Object Lesson: Be a Friend

You will need one wooden craft stick per child, plus 8 more. Before class, draw a sad face on the end of each child's stick. Draw happy faces on the 8 extra sticks. Ask the children if there is anyone they know in school who doesn't seem to have any friends. Perhaps this child walks around the playground all alone. Many times, new students feel left out. Also, sometimes kids who are handicapped or who look different from other people are often left out. Maybe some of the children, and even you, have felt that way at some time—wanting to be liked and included, but being left out. Tell the children that if everyone loved others like Jesus does, everyone would have lots of friends! Then hand each child a craft stick with a sad face. Ask the children if they can break theirs in half. (They should be able to break them easily.) Explain to the children that when one person is left out and is lonely, he or she feels broken inside and kind of sad. Then show the children the 8 smiley face sticks. Call them "friends." Bind the 8 sticks together with a rubber band and hand the bundle to a child. Ask the child if he or she can break the bundle of sticks. The child won't be able to. Let others try, too. Then tell the children that when kids play together, like each other, and include everyone in the group, each child is a stronger person and everyone is happy! Tell the children to start watching the people around them. If they see someone without a friend, tell them to get some friends to go with them and invite the child to play or to sit by them at lunch. They can be a friend and gain a friend! That's what Jesus would do!

Unit 10

Activities for Loving Everyone

Game: Web of Love

Bring to class a ball of yarn, any color. Have the children stand in a circle with you. Tell them you are going to make a spider web. As you hold the end of the string in your hand, throw the ball of yarn across the circle to one of the children. Say something nice about that child. Tell the children that they will do the same thing, taking turns throwing the yarn back and forth to one person at a time until everyone has had the yarn. The child throwing the yarn says something nice about the one who catches it. After they have finished throwing the yarn back and forth around the circle, it will look like a big spider web!

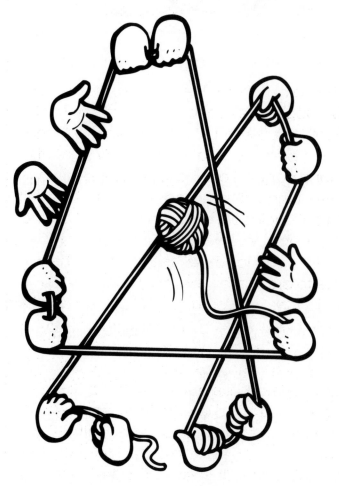

Craft: "Thumbbody" Loves You

Have each child make a card to send to an elderly person who is in a nursing home or who is a shut-in at home. Talk to the children about elderly people who are lonely because they cannot get out and visit other people. You will need to provide some ink pads (washable ink), construction paper, and markers. Have the children fold their papers in half like a greeting card. On the front of their cards, have them design a picture using inked thumbprints, like the ones on this page. Show them the examples, but encourage them to make their own pictures and designs. Some designs will need to be finished with a marker. Inside the card, have them write, *"Thumbbody" loves you. I do, and God does, too!* Make sure they sign their names. Help the children get their cards delivered.

Woman at the Well

One day, Jesus was traveling through the region of Samaria. He came to a well that had been there for many, many years. It was called Jacob's well. (Jacob was the grandson of Abraham, and the son of Isaac, whom we read about in the Old Testament.) Jesus sat down at the well to rest. His disciples had gone into town to buy food.

A Samaritan woman came to the well to draw water. Jesus asked her, "Will you give me a drink?"

The Samaritan woman said, "You are a Jew. I am a Samaritan woman. How can you ask me for a drink?"

The reason the woman asked this was because most Jews would not have anything to do with Samaritans. Sometimes Jews would travel many extra miles on a different road to avoid even passing through Samaria. Samaritans were a mixed breed of people. They were mixed because many years earlier, a king had sent people from foreign countries to live in the region of Samaria. They married some of the Israelites (Jews) who lived there. Under the Law of Moses, it was a sin for an Israelite to marry a foreigner because they often worshiped idols. Through the years, this mixed race of people came to be hated by many of the Jews.

(Continued on the next page.)

Woman at the Well

Jesus answered her, *"If you knew the gift of God and who it is that asks you for a drink, you would have asked him and he would have given you living water."* (John 4:10) By saying this, Jesus was talking about eternal life.

She asked, "Where can you get this living water? Are you greater than Jacob who gave us this well and drank from it himself?"

They talked some more, and then the Samaritan woman told Jesus that she knew that some day the Messiah (Christ) would come. Then Jesus told her that He was the Messiah!

Meanwhile, Jesus' disciples came back from town and were surprised to see Him talking to the woman, but no one dared to ask, "Why are you talking to her?"

The woman left her water jar there and went back to town. She told everyone what Jesus had said to her. "Could this be the Christ?" she asked.

The Samaritan people came to the well to see Jesus for themselves. Many of them believed in Him. They asked Jesus to stay with them, and He did for two days. The Samaritans believed because of what the woman told them and also because they heard Jesus' themselves. They said, "We know that this man truly is the Savior of the world."

Talk About It

- What race of people did many of the Jews hate?

- Why did the woman act surprised that Jesus was speaking to her?

- Why are some people mean to others who are different from them?

- Does God love everyone the same, regardless of their color of their skin or where they come from?

- Who should you love?

Unit 10

Brotherly Love

Name _____

Do you love God? Do you love all people? To find out what the Bible says about loving God and loving people, fill in the missing words in the Bible verse below by looking at the clues. Use both clues to find the correct word in the Answer Box. Write the correct words in the blanks. The first one is done for you.

Answer Box			
	brother	whom	seen
	given	love	John
	command	anyone	God

"For ___anyone___ who does not _____ his

_____, _____ he has _____, cannot

_____ _____, _____ he has not

_____. And he has _____ us this _____:

Whoever loves _____ must also _____ his

_____." (1 _____ 4: 20–21)

Unit

10

I Love You

Name _____

Listed below are some of the people whom you should love. Find them in the puzzle going up, down, forward, backward, and diagonally. Highlight or circle your answers. (Hint: Two of the words are inside two other words!)

all races
brothers
cousins
enemies
father
friends
God
grandfather
grandmother
handicapped
Jesus
mother
neighbor
sisters
the poor

```
T  M  Z  Y  G  C  O  U  S  I  N  S
O  H  D  S  R  E  T  S  I  S  A  C
F  H  A  U  A  V  K  L  U  U  L  B
Z  J  E  N  N  X  B  R  M  S  L  R
G  R  A  N  D  F  A  T  H  E  R  O
W  O  J  E  M  I  R  J  Z  J  A  T
C  B  V  U  O  N  C  I  Y  B  C  H
J  H  R  P  T  X  I  A  E  R  E  E
P  G  O  D  H  Z  J  C  P  N  S  R
K  I  E  N  E  M  I  E  S  P  D  S
I  E  F  X  R  C  Y  Z  B  J  E  S
B  N  Z  T  H  E  P  O  O  R  L  D
```

Now use the word list again to find the missing words in the Bible verses below.

1. Love your n_____ as yourself. (Matthew 19:19)

2. Love the Lord your G_____. (Luke 10:27)

3. Love your e_____. (Luke 6:35)

4. Honor your f_____ and m_____. (Matthew 15:4)

Faraway Friends

"Today in Bible class, we are going to choose pen pals from several different countries," said Mrs. Wylie. "Our missionaries around the world have sent us names of some of the children who attend church services with them. So draw a name from the box. Then make your pen pal a card. Draw a picture of yourself, and write about who you are. You may ask your pen pal questions in your letter, too," she said.

Mrs. Wylie let Holly choose first. "I got a girl from Germany," said Holly. "I wish I could go there and visit her!"

"My pen pal is from Egypt," Kristy said. "I wonder if she lives near the Nile River! Where is your pen pal from, Lexie?"

"London, England!" Lexie exclaimed. The other children drew names from faraway places, too. It was exciting to imagine getting a letter in return from a pen pal in another country.

As the children were making their cards, Mrs. Wylie told the class, "God loves everyone. He wants us to love everyone, too, no matter what color they are or what country they live in." She read Matthew 28:19 which says that Jesus told His followers to go and make disciples of all nations.

(Continued on the next page.)

Faraway Friends

After class was over, Holly, Kristy, and Lexie went to get a drink. Just then, Kayla walked by. Holly said, "Oh, I can't stand that Kayla. Just because she is older than we are, she thinks she is so cool."

"I know," Lexie said. "She was talking about me behind my back last week. One of her friends told me. It really hurt my feelings. I hate her."

"Me, too," said Kristy. "She's always making fun of the way I talk. She makes me so mad!"

Mrs. Wylie was waiting in line behind the girls to get a drink. "I couldn't help but hear what you were saying, girls," she said. "You know, in class today, we talked about loving people from other countries. You were all so excited about your pen pals. You showed love to them by making them pretty cards. But you aren't showing love to someone who lives right here and goes to church with you. Maybe you think of Kayla as your enemy, but God says to love your enemies and pray for them."

Holly, Kristy, and Lexie looked at each other. "You know," said Holly, "it's easier to love somebody that you have never even met than to love some people whom you know very well."

"I guess you're right," said Kristy. "I never thought about that. Let's pray for Kayla today."

Lexie added, "And let's ask God to help us love Kayla more. Like Mrs. Wylie said, 'God wants us to love everyone!'"

Talk About It
- Why was it easy for the girls to love their pen pals whom they had never met?
- Why was it hard for the girls to love Kayla?
- Why is it easy to say you love everyone, but hard to really do it?
- What if God loved everyone, except you? How would you feel?

Unit **10**

How Would You Feel?

Name _____

To truly love other people, we must imagine how they feel when others treat them in a bad way or a good way. Read each story below. How would you feel if this were you? Draw faces to show your answer.

1. Carlos was worried about the first day in his new school. He could not speak English very well. He was not sure if he would be able to understand what the teacher was saying. How would you feel if you were in this situation?

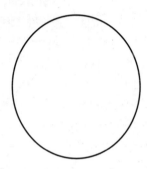

2. Jill's family decided to start going to church. Jill had a deformed hand. She wondered what the kids in her Bible class would do when they noticed it. On Sunday, she walked into the room, and a girl looked at her. She saw Jill's hand. She said, "Hi. Want to sit by me?" The teacher gave Jill a sticker for her attendance chart. A boy smiled at her as he handed out the workbooks. They treated her just like everyone else! How would you feel?

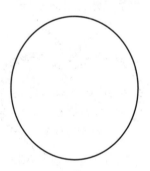

3. Doug was overweight. He was bigger than all the other children in his class. The boys said he was too fat to play basketball with them. The girls teased him and called him "Chubby." When they had races in gym class, Doug came in last, and the children laughed at him. How would you feel?

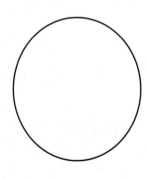

Unit **10**

My Contract

Name _____

Use a pink or red crayon to color in the hearts that tell what you can do to show love to everyone. Use a black crayon to make a big X on the hearts that do NOT tell ways to show love.

Be nice to people who are different from you.

Smile at people.

Be friendly to a new student.

Hit someone.

Say bad things about someone you don't like.

Pray for your enemies.

Care for a sick family member.

Kick someone when you are mad.

Give someone a gift.

Enjoy being with elderly people.

Give some of your toys to the poor.

Be kind to someone of another race.

Help someone in need.

Hate someone.

Tell your friends not to like someone.

Fight and argue.

Hope something bad happens to someone.

Make fun of a handicapped person.

If you want to make a commitment to love everyone, copy the sentence below. Then sign your name and write the date.

 I promise to do my best to love everyone.

_____

 Signed _____

Date _____

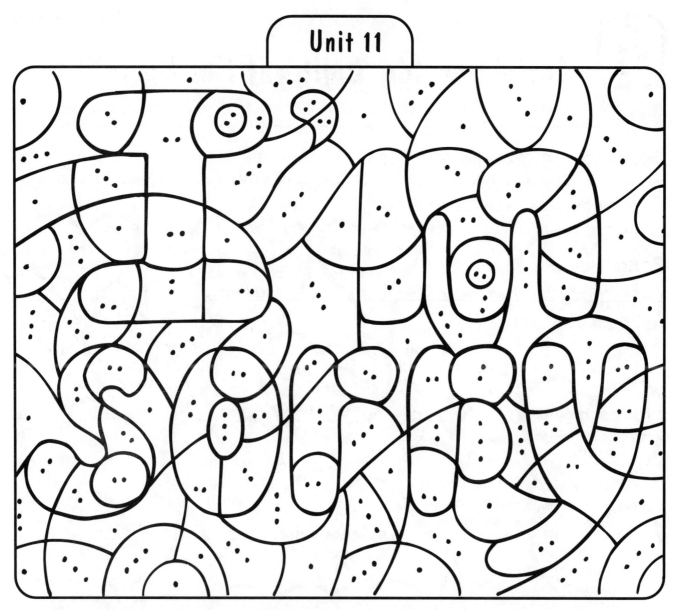

To find the hidden words in the puzzle above color in only the spaces that have two dots in them. Always remember to say these magic words when you need to.

To be sorry means . . .
- to admit you are wrong
- to apologize
- to take the blame for something you did or said
- to ask for forgiveness
- to regret that you have done wrong

- to want to start over
- to humble yourself
- to let go of pride and set the ecord straight
- to not be proud of doing wrong
- to not blame others

Unit 11

Activities for Saying, "I'm Sorry"

The activities below are a great way to teach children to say two very important words: "I'm sorry."

Role Playing: You Be the Star!

Divide the class into small groups or pairs. Tell each group that they will be given a few minutes to work up a simple skit to perform for the class. Each skit should be about a situation in which someone does something wrong and then says, "I'm sorry."

Song

(tune: "Have You Ever Seen a Lassie?")

I will always say, "I'm sorry,"
"I'm sorry, I'm sorry."
I will always say, "I'm sorry,"
When I have done wrong.
I'll ask for forgiveness
And I won't blame others.
I will always say, "I'm sorry,"
When I have done wrong.

Craft: Fish and Jonah Puppets

This craft will help the children review the Bible story about Jonah. Give each child a copy of the patterns on page 112 and a lunch sack. Have the children color the patterns and cut them out. Tell them to glue the top part of the fish on the bottom of the sack, right by to the edge. Then they glue the other part of the fish up against the fold, as shown. To make Jonah, have them cut two inches off the end of a pipe cleaner. Show them how to twist a loop in the middle of the long piece and add a few more twists. Next, they put the short piece of pipe cleaner across it to make the arms, and twist the long piece tightly around it, as shown. Make a few more twists. Then separate the two sides to form the legs. Read the story of Jonah on pages 113 and 114 with the children. Afterwards, let them use their two puppets to act out the story.

Unit
11

Activities for Saying, "I'm Sorry"

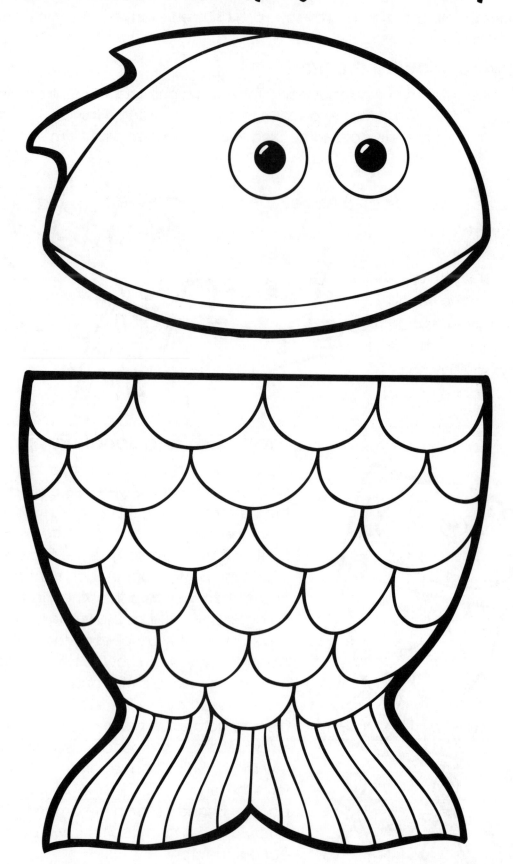

112

Jonah Learns a Lesson

In Old Testament times, God sometimes spoke directly to men. One day, God spoke to Jonah. He told Jonah to go to the city of Nineveh and tell the people there to stop being bad.

But Jonah did not obey God. He ran away and tried to hide from the Lord. Jonah should have known that it is impossible to hide from God! He got on a ship that was leaving for Tarshish. But the Lord sent a violent storm. The winds and the waves battered the ship until it was about to break apart. Jonah was on the deck below, sleeping.

The sailors were afraid for their lives. They cast lots to find out who was responsible for this dangerous situation. The lot fell on Jonah. So the sailors went and asked him, "Tell us, who is responsible for making all this trouble for us? What do you do? Where do you come from?"

He answered, "I am a Hebrew. I worship the one true God of heaven, who made the sea and the land."

This terrified the sailors. They asked him what he had done. He told them he was running away from the Lord.

(Continued on the next page.)

Unit
11

Jonah Learns a Lesson

The sea was getting rougher and rougher, so they asked him what they could do to make the sea calm down.

Jonah replied, "Throw me into the sea. I know that it is my fault that this terrible storm has occurred." Jonah took the blame and admitted that it was his fault.

When the sailors threw Jonah overboard, the sea grew calm. Then the Lord had a great fish swallow Jonah. Jonah spent three days and three nights inside the fish! Can you imagine how scared Jonah must have been?

What do you think Jonah did while he was inside the fish? He prayed to God! He was sorry that he had disobeyed God. He was sorry that he had tried to run away and hide instead of doing what God told him to do. So God commanded the fish to spit Jonah out on the shore.

Then Jonah proved that he was sorry. He went to Nineveh and preached the word of the Lord as God had told him. God forgave Jonah because he repented. To *repent* means to do something about being sorry. It means to stop doing wrong, and do what is right.

Talk About It

- Why didn't Jonah do what God asked?

- Was God mad? How do you know?

- Was Jonah sorry?

- How did Jonah show God he was sorry?

- What can you do to show someone you are sorry for something?

- How can you show God you are sorry for something?

Unit 11

How to Say, "I'm Sorry"

Name _____

Sometimes it is very hard to say, "I'm sorry." The Bible tells us to admit it when we have done wrong. It also tells us what to do next. Can you read the Bible verse below? Write it correctly on the lines.

" _____ _____ _____

_____ _____ _____

_____ _____ _____

_____." (James 5:16)

Unit **11**

One Is Sorry, One Is Not

Name _____

Jesus told a story about two men who went to the temple to pray. One was a Pharisee, a very religious man. The other was a tax collector. Tax collectors had a bad reputation for taking more money than they were supposed to and keeping it for themselves. The Pharisee stood up and prayed, "God, thank you that I am not evil like some other men—robbers, evildoers—or even like this tax collector. I fast twice a week and give you a tenth of all the money I get." That man did not ask God to forgive him of his sins, but instead bragged about himself. He also looked down on the tax collector.

The tax collector would not even look up to heaven, but prayed, "God, have mercy on me. I am a sinner." He was confessing his sins and saying, "I'm sorry." Jesus said that the tax collector, rather than the Pharisee, was forgiven. (Luke 18:9–14)

Follow the instructions below.

1. Draw a red box around the word in the story that tells who was not sorry.

2. Draw a green circle around the words in the story that tells who was sorry.

3. Draw a blue line under the name of the person who told the story.

4. Underline the correct answer: Whom did Jesus say was forgiven?

   (a) the Pharisee   (b) Peter   (c) John   (d) the tax collector

5. Why was the tax collector forgiven?

   (a) because he gave a tenth of all he had
   (b) because he was truly sorry
   (c) because he fasted twice a week
   (d) because he collected taxes

6. When you do something wrong, what should you say?

   "___ ___   ___ ___ ___ ___ ___."

Sorry, Dad!

Early Saturday morning, Dad woke Dan up. "Dan, wake up," Dad said. "I want you to clean out the garage today. Get dressed and eat your breakfast. Then get started." "Yes, sir," Dan said, then he turned over and went back to sleep.

Dad went to Julie's room and said, "Julie, wake up. We are going to do some spring cleaning today . . . the whole family. I want you to clean out the hall closet. Straighten up the books and picture albums. Throw away the trash and organize the games. Make sure all the little game pieces are back in the right boxes. It's a mess in there!"

"No, Dad! Saturday is my only morning to sleep late. I don't want to clean out closets," Julie whined.

"Do what I say, Julie," said Dad, as he walked out of the room.

Julie dragged herself out of bed and put on her clothes. She brushed her teeth and pulled her hair up into a ponytail. Then she splashed water on her face. By the time she had finished eating a bowl of cereal, she was wide awake.

(Continued on the next page.)

Unit 11

Sorry, Dad!

Julie heard Dad on the stairs. "Dad, I'm sorry I said what I did this morning. I'll clean out the closet now."

"Good girl!" said Dad, and he patted her on the back.

Julie organized the games, the books, and the picture albums. She made the closet look nice again. She even found a book that she had thought was lost. When she was finished cleaning, she sat on the floor and read it.

While Mom and Dad were cleaning out the attic, Dan kept on sleeping. Later that morning, he got up and got dressed. Then he went outside and rode his bike.

When he got home, Dad was waiting for him in the garage. "Son, why haven't you cleaned the garage like I told you to?"

"Oh, I guess I went back to sleep after you woke me up. You should have come back in there and woken me up again, Dad. Then I would have gotten up," Dan replied.

"You shouldn't blame someone else when you have done something wrong, Dan," said Dad. "So now you will not only have to clean out the garage, but you will be given an extra job to do as well."

Talk About It

• Dad told both children to do a job. Dan said, "Yes," but didn't do it. Julie said, "No," but then said she was sorry and did the job. Which one did the right thing?

• Read another story like this one that Jesus told, in Matthew 21:28-31.

• Does Jesus want you to say "I'm sorry" when you are wrong?

Unit **11**

Which Is Best?

Name _____

Look at each of the cartoons below. Which ending is best? Color only the picture that tells the correct ending.

Unit **11**

My Contract

Name _____

Use the code below to find out different ways to say, "I'm sorry." Write the sentences on the lines.

shouldn't	was	fault	apologize	me	It
wrong	I	have	Please	my	forgive

1. ⊘ ⊘ ✺ . _____

2. ⚡ ⬡ △ ✚ . _____

3. ☆ ♡ ☺ . _____

4. ⊘ ☾ . _____

5. ⊘ ⬡ ✦ . _____

If you want to make a commitment to say, "I'm sorry" when you should, copy the sentence below. Then sign your name and write the date.

I promise to do my best to say "I'm sorry" when I should.

_____

_____

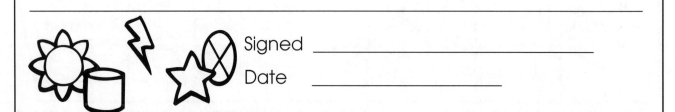

Signed _____

Date _____

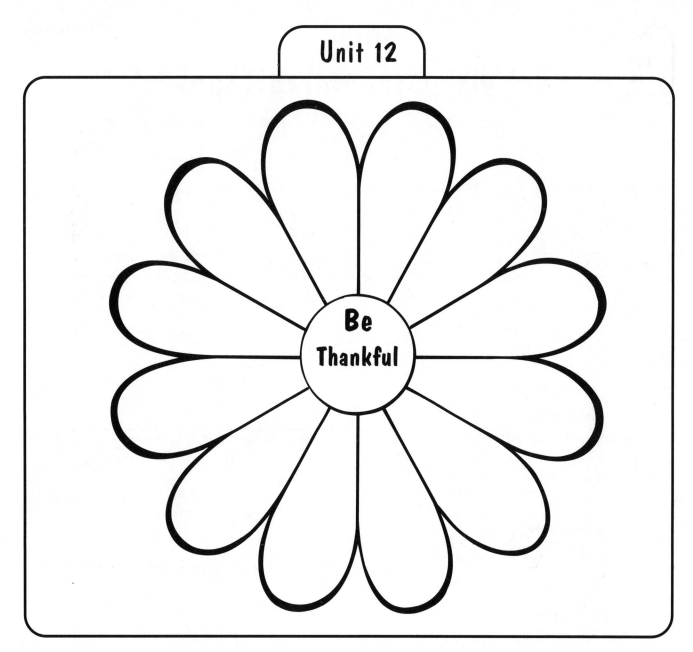

Write something that you are thankful for in each petal of the flower. Then outline the flower in bright colors.

To be thankful means . . .
- to appreciate what others do for you
- to be happy with what you have
- to be grateful
- to show good manners by saying, "Thank you"
- to honor the one who gave to you
- to feel good about a gift
- to remember to tell others that what they did for you or said about you was pleasing
- not to take something or someone for granted
- to show appreciation

Unit 12

Activities for Being Thankful

The activities below and on page 123 make it fun and easy to remind children to be thankful.

Game: Count Your Blessings

Hand each child a piece of notebook paper. Tell the children that they are going to have a contest to see who can list the most blessings from God. They must all begin at the same time and end at whatever time limit you set. Then have them count how many blessings each one listed. Let the winner read his or her list to the class first. If time allows, let the other children read their lists. Then have a moment of silent prayer, allowing the children to thank God for everything on their lists.

Song

(tune: "London Bridge")

1. Thank You, God, for Mom and Dad,
   Mom and Dad, Mom and Dad.
   Thank You, God, for Mom and Dad,
   I am very thankful.

2. Thank You, God, for pets to love . . .

3. Thank You, God, for food to eat . . .

4. Thank You, God, for clothes to wear…

5. Thank You, God, for my own house…

(Ask the children to make up more verses.)

Craft: Milk Jug Shadow Box

This craft is a fun way to help children be thankful for nature and all the beauty God made outdoors. Talk to them about the gifts of mountains, lakes, trees, and flowers. Ask them if they have ever gone camping or picnicking in a park. Tell them they are going to make shadow boxes using milk jugs. Each child needs a gallon-sized milk jug. Use sharp scissors to cut each clean, dry jug in two, about halfway down. Then give each child a copy of page 123 and help them follow the directions. (*Note:* Instead of waiting for white glue to dry, you could use a glue gun to glue the items to the children's shadow boxes.)

Unit
12

Activities for Being Thankful

Nature Shadow Box

1. Color the picture and cut it out.

2. Glue it to the inside bottom of the milk carton.

3. On the bottom of the picture, glue a little Easter grass or some paper grass. Then add very small rocks and tiny silk flowers or plants around the edges, leaving the center area open so that the picture can be seen easily.

4. Hold the top of the carton to the bottom of the carton, while your teacher tapes them together with a long piece of duct tape.

5. Color the banner "Thank You, God, for nature" and glue it over the duct tape on the side of the jug. Then peek through the opening of the jug to see what's inside.

Thank You, God, for nature.

Only One Said, "Thank You"

As Jesus traveled from town to town, He preached to the people and often healed those who were sick. Sometimes He healed people who had leprosy. Leprosy was a terrible disease that ate away at the skin. Some who got leprosy were covered with painful sores.

According to the Law of Moses, people who had leprosy had to live alone, outside the town. They had to wear torn clothes, let their hair be uncombed, and cover the lower part of their face. They had to warn others that they had leprosy by calling out, "Unclean! Unclean!" Imagine how they must have felt! Not only were they sick, but they were cut off from their family and friends. They were outcasts.

One day, while Jesus was on His way to Jerusalem, He traveled along the border between the region of Samaria and the region of Galilee. As Jesus was walking toward a village, 10 men who had leprosy met Him. They stood at a distance and called out in a loud voice, "Jesus, Master, have pity on us!"

(Continued on the next page.)

Unit
12

Only One Said, "Thank You"

Jesus did have pity on them. He was willing to heal them of their disease. He told them to show themselves to the priests. (That was what people were supposed to do if they got well. Then the priest would pronounce them clean, and they could go back into the town.)

As they went, they were healed! One of the men was a Samaritan. When he saw that he was healed, he went back to find Jesus. He praised God in a loud voice. He threw himself at Jesus' feet and thanked him.

Jesus asked him, "Were not all ten healed? Where are the others? None of the others have returned to give praise to God except this foreigner?"

Then Jesus said to the man, "Go. Your faith has healed you."

Talk About It

• Jesus healed 10 men, but only one remembered to say, "Thank you." Why do you think the other nine men didn't say "Thank you"?

• What should you do if you forget to say, "Thank you"?

• What do you thank God for each day?

Unit 12

Hidden Pictures

Name _____

God is our Father, and He takes care of us. He gives us everything we need. We must always remember to tell God, "Thank you!" There are 10 things hidden in the picture below for which we should be thankful. Circle each one as you find it. When you have finished, say a prayer, thanking God for each of those things.

"For everything God created is good, and nothing is to be rejected if it is received with thanksgiving." (1 Timothy 4:4)

Unit 12

Decode the Message

Name _____

Why is it important to be thankful? Find out by using the code below to discover what letters should go in the blanks. Write the letters, and then read the Bible verse that tells about being thankful.

A	C	D	E	F	G	H	I	J	K	L	M	N	O	R	S	T	U	V	W	Y
✸	✳	❄	✶	❋	✱	✳	✴	✵	✺	●	○	■	◻	▢	▲	▼	◆	❖	◗	❙

"____ _____ __ ___
  ✶ ✳ ❖ ✳   ▼ ✳ ✸ ■ ✳ ▲   ✳ ■   ✸ ● ●

_____, ___ ____
✳ ✳ ◻ ✳ ◆ ○ ▲ ▼ ✸ ■ ✳ ✳ ▲   ❄ ◻ ◻   ▼ ✳ ✳ ▲

,
__ __ _____ ____ ___ ___
✳ ▲   ✶ ◻ ✳ ▲   ◗ ✶ ● ●   ❄ ◻ ◻   ❙ ◻ ◆

____ _____ _____." (1 Thessalonians 5:18)
✳ ■   ✶ ✳ ◻ ✶ ▲ ▼   ✶ ✳ ▲ ◆ ▲

Unit 12 — Don't Forget to Say, "Thank You!"

Mike and Kelly were so excited about going to Grandpa and Grandma's Christmas party. Their aunts and uncles and cousins would be there. Grandma would cook a big turkey dinner, pumpkin pies, and German chocolate cake, Mike's favorite.

When they got there, Grandpa built a big fire in the fireplace because it was a cold, windy day. The Christmas tree was twinkling with lights and colorful ornaments. Christmas music was playing throughout the house.

Mike and Kelly went to look at the gifts under the tree. Kelly got a big smile on her face when she saw a very, very big present that read "To Kelly, From Grandma and Grandpa." Mike shook his present, and it rattled. What could it be? There were also presents from their cousins and aunts and uncles.

It seemed like it would never be time to open presents. Finally, after dinner, when all the dishes were washed, it was time! Kelly opened her big gift first. It was a playhouse that looked like a castle! She squealed and opened every door and window.

Mike opened his gift next. It was a remote control car, just like he had hoped for. He ran to the kitchen and tried it out. He made it go back and forth, under chairs and around in circles. What a great present it was!

(Continued on the next page.)

Unit 12 Don't Forget to Say, "Thank You!"

Then they opened their other gifts. Kelly got skates, baby dolls, a Super Bake Oven, and a book. Mike got two video games, a model airplane, a race car set, and a football. They played with their toys until time to go home.

When they got home, Mom and Dad gathered up all their gifts and put them away in the closet. "What are you doing?" asked Mike and Kelly.

"You two got a lot of nice gifts today, but you forgot to say "thank you." You were so busy playing with your new things or opening other gifts, that you never stopped to tell Grandma and Grandpa "thank you" for your playhouse and remote control car. You didn't thank your aunts and uncles and cousins for the gifts they gave you, either. It is good manners to say "thank you" when someone does something nice for you or gives you something." Then Dad said, "We will keep your new toys in the closet until you finish writing thank-you notes to every person who gave you a gift."

Mike and Kelly felt bad. They hadn't even realized that they had forgotten to say "thank you." They went upstairs and wrote their notes. Then they felt better. The next day, Mom and Dad gave them their gifts back.

Two days later, it was Christmas Day. Mike and Kelly opened their gifts from Santa and from Mom and Dad. This time, they hugged their parents and thanked them for each gift. Mom and Dad thanked Mike and Kelly for the gifts they had given them, too.

Mike even went to the window and looked up in the sky and said, "Thank you, too, Santa Claus!" Everyone laughed.

Talk About It

- Why do you think Mike and Kelly forgot to say "thank you" at the Christmas party? Has that ever happened to you?

- What did Mom and Dad do to teach Mike and Kelly a lesson?

- Have you ever written a thank-you note to someone?

- Why is it important to always say "thank you"?

Unit
12

Think About It

Name _____

What if you forgot to thank people for what they gave you? What if they took everything back? Would this happen to you?

Remember to always to say "thank you." Think about this: What if God took away everything that you have not thanked Him for? What would you be missing today? Circle anything you have forgotten to thank God for. Thank Him today for these things! Say a prayer and thank God for all the things you enjoy.

Unit
12

My Contract

Name _____

Everyone likes to be appreciated for what they do. Sometimes we do appreciate others, but we don't ever tell them. This week, try this: Thank some of the people listed below. Tell them that you appreciate what they do. You can write them a note, or just tell them. Watch their faces when you thank them! It's fun! You are sure to see a smile. It works every time!

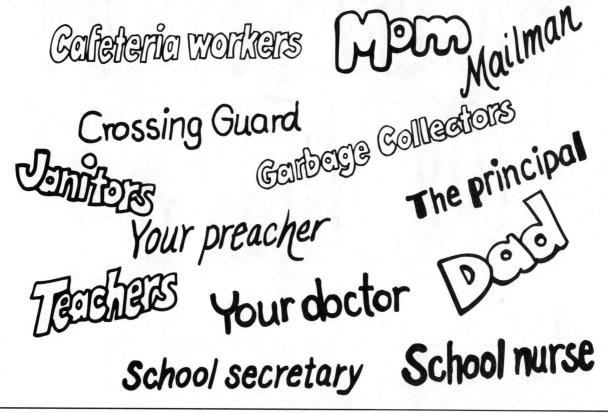

Cafeteria workers   Mom   Mailman
Crossing Guard   Garbage Collectors
Janitors   The principal
Your preacher   Dad
Teachers   Your doctor
School secretary   School nurse

If you want to make a commitment to be more thankful, copy the sentence below. Then sign your name and write the date.

I promise to do my best to be more thankful.

_____

_____

Signed _____

Date _____

SHARE WITH OTHERS

Let the children at each table take turns coloring the letters above. Then decorate the box with a pretty border.

To share with others means . . .

- to let others use or have what is yours
- to give up something when there is not enough for everyone
- to be generous with what you have
- to give to others who are needy

- to show charity
- to give to a worthy cause
- to participate in the needs of others
- to not be selfish or stingy
- to not keep everything to yourself

Unit 13

Activities for Sharing With Others

Sharing can be lots of fun for children when they complete the activities below and on page 134.

Craft: Charity Posters

Before class, purchase a package of play money at a toy store or a discount store. Then provide the children with construction paper, markers, crayons, and old magazines. Each child will also need a sheet of posterboard. Tell the children to create a poster using the play money and the other materials. The posters should encourage others to share with those in need. Display the posters somewhere in your church building for others to see. (Optional— Have a contest to determine the best poster and to raise money for missions or a special project. Perhaps you could ask church members to drop pennies, nickels, or dimes into paper cups that are in front of each poster. The poster with the most money wins, and all the proceeds are given to a charity.)

Object Lesson: Share a Snack

Bring in some graham crackers, chocolate bars, or any kind of snack that is easily divided. Give everyone a napkin. Tell the children that they are going to have a snack. Let someone lead the prayer to thank God for the food. Then only put on the plate half as many graham crackers (or snack) as there are children, and place them in the center of the table. Tell the children that there is not enough for everyone, and that you suppose that some of them will get a snack, and some of them won't. After they react to that, ask them how they could solve this problem so that it is fair to everyone.

Unit 13

Activities for Sharing With Others

Song

(tune: "B-I-N-G-O")

1. I have clothes and toys and food,
   So I will share with others,
   S-H-A-R-E,
   S-H-A-R-E,
   S-H-A-R-E,
   I will share with others.

2. I know the Lord wants me to give . . .

3. Some for me and some for you . . .

Class Project: Clothing Drive

Ask the children if they have any clothes at home that they have outgrown or don't wear anymore and that they are willing to share. Send a note home with the children explaining the project. Tell the children that they must get permission from their parents to bring in their old clothes. The children can bring their donations in a box or paper sack. Remind them not to bring stained or torn clothing. Tell them that if they don't wear it anymore because it is stained or torn, no one else would want to either. Explain that the clothes should be clean and folded neatly. Make a decision ahead of time where you will send the clothing—perhaps to a missionary, an orphanage, a family in need, a shelter, or a resale shop for the needy. Praise the children for sharing with the needy. Ask them how it makes them feel to share. (*Note*: This could also be done as a food drive or toy drive, depending on the needs in your church or town.)

A Boy Shared His Lunch

One day, Jesus was teaching a large crowd of people out in the country. He was also healing those who were sick.

Late in the afternoon, Jesus' twelve disciples came to Him and said, "Send the people away so they can go to the local villages to find food."

But Jesus said, "You give them something to eat."

The disciples were surprised that Jesus said that because there were about 5,000 men there that day, as well as women and children. It was a huge crowd!

Philip, one of the disciples, said, "It would take more than eight months' wages to buy enough bread for everyone!"

Jesus said, "How many loaves do you have? Go and see."

Andrew, another of Jesus' disciples, said, "There is a boy with five, small barley loaves and two, small fish. But how far will these go among so many?"

(Continued on the next page.)

Unit 13

A Boy Shared His Lunch

The little boy gave his lunch to Jesus. Then Jesus had the people sit in groups on the grass. Taking the five loaves and two fish, Jesus looked up to heaven and said a prayer to thank God for the food. Then He broke the loaves and gave them to the disciples to set before the people. He also gave them the fish. But now, there were no longer only five loaves of bread, and only two fish . . . there was enough for the whole crowd! It was a miracle!

Everyone ate until they were no longer hungry. Jesus said to His disciples, "Gather the pieces that are left over. Let nothing be wasted."

So the disciples picked up twelve baskets full of broken pieces of bread and fish. There were more leftovers than the food they had started with! The lunch that the little boy shared with Jesus became enough food for a whole crowd!

Talk About It

- Who shared his lunch with Jesus? Who did Jesus share the lunch with?

- How many baskets full of leftover pieces did the disciples pick up?

- Can you make one little lunch become enough food to feed over 5,000 people? How was Jesus able to do it?

- Tell about a time when you shared with someone. How did it make you feel?

- Tell about a time when someone shared with you. How did it make you feel?

Unit
13

Which One Doesn't Belong?

Name _____

God wants us to share our blessings with others. In each set of boxes below, there are three things that you should share, but one thing doesn't belong. Mark an X on the things that don't belong. Then color the pictures of the things that you should share.

"Share with God's people who are in need . . ." (Romans 12:13)

Unit
13

Everyone Shared

Name _____

When the church first began, all the believers were united like one big happy family. Acts 4:32 tells us what they did. To find out, cut out each puzzle piece, and arrange all of the pieces correctly. Then, glue them onto a piece of construction paper.

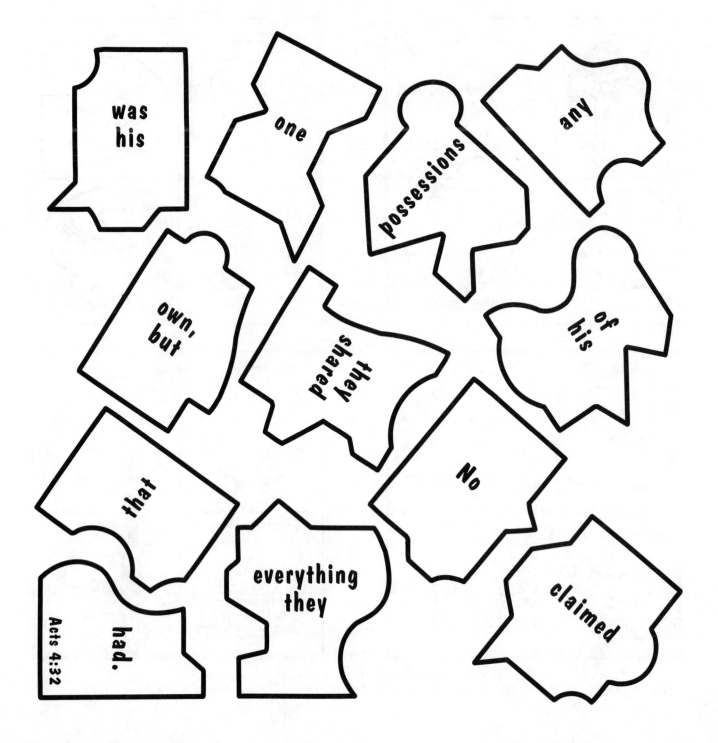

Unit
13

A Lesson on Sharing

Taylor spent the night at Lexie's house. About 10:00 the next morning, Lexie's Aunt Melissa called. Melissa had twin boys who were three years old. They were Lexie's cousins. "Hello, Lexie?" Aunt Melissa said. "Could you come over and watch Matt and Mark for a little while? I want to sew some curtains today, and I don't want Matt and Mark to get into the pins and scissors and all. Could you play with the boys for a few hours?"

"Okay," said Lexie, "but my friend, Taylor, spent the night with me last night. So, is it alright if she comes, too?"

"Sure! That's fine!" Aunt Melissa said.

At Aunt Melissa's house, Matt and Mark played with their toy cars. "Give me that red car!" said Matt.

"No, it's mine," said Mark.

"No, mine!" yelled Matt. They both pulled on the car until Matt won. Mark got mad and hit his brother.

"Stop that!" said Lexie. "You have to share. Here, Mark, you play with the green car for a while. Then you and Matt can switch cars later."

(Continued on the next page.)

A Lesson on Sharing

Then Taylor and Lexie poured the boys some juice in cups with lids on them. "I want the cup with the tiger on it!" said Mark. "No, that's my cup!" said Matt, as he grabbed it out of Mark's hand. Mark wailed, "I had it first!"

"Don't fight, boys," said Taylor. "You have to take turns. Today, Mark can have the tiger cup, and tomorrow, you can have it, Matt."

Lexie shook her head and said to Taylor, "They need to learn to share!"

When Aunt Melissa finished the curtains, she took Lexie and Taylor home. Aunt Melissa and the boys came inside when Lexie's mom invited them to stay for supper.

"Let's go up to my room and play my new video game, okay?" Lexie said to Taylor. "I'll go first."

Taylor asked, "Can't two players play at the same time?"

"No, this is a one-player game," said Lexie.

Taylor watched as Lexie played. When the game ended, Taylor said, "Ok, it's my turn."

"No, not yet. I almost got to the next level. I'm going to play one more time," Lexie said. "Hey, that's not fair," Taylor said, angrily, "it's my turn!" Taylor reached for the controls, and Lexie jerked them away from her. "Stop!" she said. They were both pulling on the controls when Matt and Mark appeared in the doorway.

"You have to take turns," said Matt. Then Mark added, "You need to learn to share."

Lexie and Taylor looked at each other and laughed. "I guess they taught us a lesson, didn't they!" Lexie said, as she handed the controls to Taylor.

Talk About It

- What lesson did Lexie and Taylor teach the boys?

- What lesson did the boys teach Lexie and Taylor?

- When is it fun to share? When is it hard to share?

- Read Hebrews 13:16. What does the Bible say about sharing?

Unit 13

If You Were President

Name _____

Suppose you were President of the United States. You saw that many Americans had plenty of money, food, clothing, houses, and cars. You also saw that other Americans did not have jobs or enough food to eat or clothes to wear. These people couldn't afford a house of their own or a car to drive. You decide to pass a Sharing Law so that everyone will have plenty. Write what your law would say. Draw a picture to go with your law. Then sign your name and write the date.

SHARING LAW OF AMERICA

Signed _____

Date _____

Unit
13

My Contract

Name _____

Color the books that tell ways to share with others.

If you want to make a commitment to share with others, copy the sentence below. Then sign your name and write the date.

 I promise to do my best to share with others.

_____

_____

Signed _____

Date _____

Answer Key

Page 8

Cross shape reads: "'Love the Lord your God with all your heart and with all your soul and with all your mind.'"

Page 9

1. earth, people, revere
2. Shout, earth, gladness, songs, God, made
3. love, strength

Page 13

Answers going down each column:
√, X, √, √, X, √, √, X, X, √, √, √, X, √

God, glory, honor, created

Page 18

"Do to others as you would have them do to you." (Luke 6:31)

Page 19

". . . Honor one another above yourselves." (Romans 12:10)
"(Therefore) as we have (opportunity) let us do good to all people . . ." (Galatians 6:10)

Page 22

BE FAIR!

Page 23

Lines should connect to: Cooperate. Use good manners. Take turns. Let someone else go first. Honor people older than you. Be fair to everyone.

Page 29

In each square, the top and the bottom sections are true. The others are false.

Page 30

1. tell you the truth
2. tell you the truth
3. tell you the truth

Page 33

1. lie
2. truth
3. truth
4. lie

Page 34

It makes God happy when I tell the truth.

Page 40

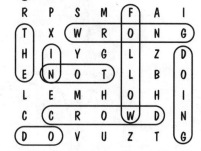

Do not follow the crowd in doing wrong. (Exodus 23:2)

Page 41

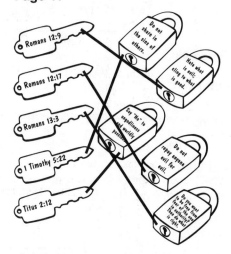

Page 44

1. red
2. green
3. red
4. red
5. green
6. green
7. red

Page 45

I will behave in public. I will use my manners. I will mind my parents. I will do what's right. I will not break the rules. I will try not to get in trouble.

Page 51

1. *"Whoever is kind to the needy honors God."*
2. *"Love is kind."*
3. *"Be kind…to one another."*

Page 52

1. They brought him to Jesus to be healed.
2. Jesus healed him and forgave him of his sins.

Page 55

J, E, S, U, S; JESUS

Page 56

1. smile
2. frown
3. smile
4. smile
5. frown
6. smile
7. smile
8. smile
9. frown
10. smile

Page 62

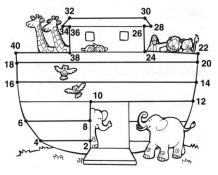

food, his wife, his 3 sons, his sons' wives

Page 63

1. hand
2. talk
3. red
4. house
5. Bible
6. street
7. mouth
8. play
9. Brush
10. Sit

Page 66

1. C
2. D
3. B
4. A

Page 67

(Answers may vary.)
1st wheel: People to obey.
2nd wheel: School Rules.

Page 73

1. against
2. do
3. forgive
4. heavenly
5. if
6. men
7. sins
8. when
9. you

"For if you forgive men when they sin against you, your heavenly Father will also forgive you. But if you do not forgive men their sins, your Father will not forgive your sins." (Matthew 6:14–15)

Answer Key

Page 74

"'Do not seek revenge or bear a grudge against one of your people, but love your neighbor as yourself.'" (Leviticus 19:18)

Page 78

Correct answers are at these positions: 12:00, 2:00, 3:00, 4:00, 6:00, 9:00, 10:00, 11:00

Page 83

1. dream
2. brothers
3. prisoners
4. plan
5. Pharaoh
6. grain
7. sheep
8. Potiphar
9. responsible
10. wife
11. slave
12. famine
13. plenty
14. Egypt

RESPONSIBILITY

Page 84

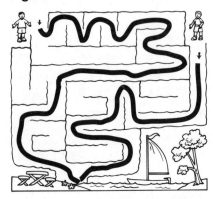

Page 88

Keep my room clean.; Do my homework.; Do what my parents say to do.; Do a good job.; Mind my manners.; Always be on time.; Take good care of my things.; Do what's right.

Page 93

"BE COMPLETELY HUMBLE AND GENTLE; BE PATIENT, BEARING WITH ONE ANOTHER IN LOVE." (Ephesians 4:2)

Page 94

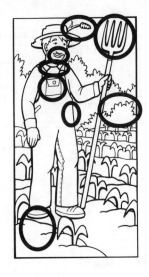

Page 98

Relax. Be tolerant. Remain calm. Chill out! Give people time. Handle a delay easily. Wait without complaining.

Page 104

anyone, love, brother, whom, seen, love, God, whom, seen, given, command, God, love, brother, John

Page 105

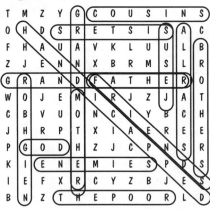

1. neighbor
2. God
3. enemies
4. father, mother

Page 108

1. scared face
2. happy face
3. sad face

Page 109

Color pink or red: Be nice to people who are different from you.; Smile at people.; Be friendly to a new student.; Pray for your enemies.; Enjoy being with elderly people.; Give some of your toys to the poor.; Give someone a gift.; Help someone in need.; Be kind to someone of another race.; Care for a sick family member.

Page 115

Therefore confess your sins to each other and pray for each other.

Page 116

1. Pharisee
2. tax collector
3. Jesus
4. D
5. B
6. I'm sorry

Page 119

1. B
2. B
3. A

Page 120

1. I shouldn't have.
2. It was my fault.
3. Please forgive me.
4. I apologize.
5. I was wrong.

Page 126

Page 127

Give thanks in all circumstances, for this is God's will for you in Christ Jesus. (I Thessalonians 5:18)

Page 137

X's on: child blowing nose, alligator, storm cloud, giraffe

Page 138

No one claimed that any of his possessions was his own, but they shared everything they had. Acts 4:32

Page 142

All should be colored except: Fight over whose turn it is.; Be selfish and greedy.; Keep everything to yourself.